My Feet Need Washing, Too

My Feet Need Washing, Too

Timothy N. Sharpe

REVIEW AND HERALD® PUBLISHING ASSOCIATION
WASHINGTON, DC 20039-0555
HAGERSTOWN, MD 21740

Copyright © 1990 by
Review and Herald® Publishing Association

The author assumes full responsibility for the accuracy of all facts
and quotations as cited in this book.

This book was
Edited by Gerald Wheeler
Designed by Bill Kirstein
Type set: Goudy Old Style

PRINTED IN U.S.A.

94 93 92 91 90   10 9 8 7 6 5 4 3 2 1

Library of Congress Cataloging in Publication Data

Sharpe, Timothy N., 1943-
   My feet need washing, too / Timothy N. Sharpe.
     p.   cm.
   1. Seventh-day Adventists—Clergy. 2. Adventists—Clergy.
3. Clergy—Office. 4. Pastoral theology—Seventh-day Adventists.
5. Sharpe. timothy N., 1943-   .   I. Title.
BX6154.S47   1990
253'.2—dc20   89-29815
                                                                                  CIP

ISBN 0-8280-0549-4

Read Me First
(Introduction)

The immoral escapades of several "tele-evangelists" and other clergymen has marred the image of the ministry. The world in general does not now trust those who have set themselves up as religious authorities. The Seventh-day Adventist Church also faces some of these same problems.

We live in a changing world. When I began my service for God and the church, a minister automatically had the respect of his congregation. When a person took such a position of leadership, the church members assumed that he was called of God. Today, when I am assigned a church, I find that I have to prove my calling. In and of itself this is not a bad thing. The problem comes when I as a minister begin to look at my church the same way, asking even before I know them, Do these members really love Jesus and the church? I now find myself waiting to see how a member acts before I trust him, no matter what church office he holds.

In this great church, I see a need for the lay member and the pastor to understand each other better within our changing roles. We need such discernment in order for mutual respect to develop.

The one thing that has remained constant over the years is the success that can come when a congregation and their minister work together. The pastor needs the congregation, and the congregation the pastor. Most of all, we need to love each other in Christ's love.

A minister often leads a lonely life. A congregation may get to know their pastor, may learn to love him very much, but circumstances raise certain barriers between him and them. The sad thing is that the minister may not always be able to explain why he did certain things or why certain things happened. He may not be allowed to tell of his joys and his sorrows. Many times such situations can create distrust. How can we fix this?

This book seeks to let the congregation know about some of the things that have gone on in my ministry, things I have not always been able to tell others about until now. In some of these areas I have had great success, while in others I have failed. I hope that you, the reader, will see that we in the ministry are real people—human people. We do not always have the answers. Many times we do not even know what the questions are. But if we love God, He will take our feeble efforts and bless them.

I assure you that the people in these stories are real people. Naturally I have changed their names—and some of the facts—in order to protect their identity. My prayer is that all of us will be able to accept each other to present a united front to this world. May we find ourselves working together as ministers for Christ.

Signed, Pastor Timothy N. Sharpe

My Feet
Need Washing, Too

To most people that day it appeared to be a normal Communion Sabbath. I preached the sermon and led the men into the room where we were to wash each others' feet. My son, Tim, stood quietly by the door as the elders and I passed. Our eyes met.

"Do you have anyone to serve you yet?"

Tim shook his head.

As we washed each other's feet, those looking on could tell we were having an emotional experience. We held an intimate and private conversation. They watched as we embraced and held onto each other. It is always nice to observe a father and son participate in Communion together. A few minutes later I stood in front of the congregation, leading them in partaking of the emblems of Jesus' broken body.

The people shook my hand as they left the sanctuary. Several of them praised God for the beautiful service. In the quiet moment after the last member had gone by, an elder started talking to me.

"Pastor, the Holy Spirit must have been at work here today. I really felt good about the whole service. I think the people felt good about what happened here, too. God really used you. . . ." He continued to talk, but I had quit listening.

The Holy Spirit had indeed been at work, but not in the way he thought.

It had been a terrible week for me. Committee meetings, marriage counseling, problems in the church school, and all the other chores a minister is supposed to do had sapped my energy. Planning for the Communion service should be one of the easiest things a minister does. That week it had been extremely hard.

I had some highly emotional members who never felt blessed unless my stories and illustrations led them to tears. They needed a soul-stirring presentation. Others in the congregation prided themselves on their thought processes. They had to be enlightened and challenged in their thinking. I just couldn't get the proper balance for the sermon.

Some of the members who needed the Communion service the most would be attending other churches that day. I secretly wished that I could visit, too, or at least get someone to have the service for me.

When I had responsibility for three churches I had tried to get a local elder to conduct the service in at least one of the churches. In most cases, though, they preferred not to. Even when I would ask a guest speaker to preside at Communion, he would decline as well. "The people really like to hear their own pastor for that service." I've heard those words many times.

My worries that morning also included time. How much past twelve o'clock would it run today? Communion always takes longer than a "regular" service. So often I found myself hurrying from one church to another and from one part of the service to the next, trying not to be confused, trying to get a blessing from it.

I tried hard to please everyone. Unfortunately for me, the ceremony today had become just a ritual that had to be endured.

Things should have been so much better today. I now had responsibility for only one congregation. My children had not yet betrayed any family secrets to the public. Why was this Sabbath—this special Sabbath—so bad?

I had made excuses and had tried to blame the members.

Between Sabbath School and church I had gotten caught in the hall. The public address man wanted his grievances heard by someone in authority. He threatened to resign because the Sabbath School superintendent hadn't told him early enough that she needed extra mikes for her program. Before I could get into the pastor's study, the head deacon began to give me his latest news. The church janitor had not cleaned the Cradle Roll room well enough to suit the leader.

"Something has to be done before next week!" he demanded. "Oh, yea, I almost forgot, two of the deacons who practiced last night, aren't here today."

"Can't you get someone else?" I was getting impatient.

"That's what I'm trying to tell you," he now echoed my tone of voice. "The two replacements are the new deacons and they have not served at Communion before. I was going to work them in next time but . . . they'll do all right, just make sure you don't do anything different."

As I waited in the pastor's study, only one elder was on time. The second elder rushed in and handed me the list of visitors for the day. I didn't recognize all of the names. Would they all be familiar with Communion? Would the sermon make sense to those who had never attended an Adventist Communion service?

I preached on the attitude of the disciples at the Last Supper, how they were trying to get the best places for themselves. True Christian love, I had told the congregation, would lay aside differences, and each would serve the other. Even if you had a reason to be upset with others, you had to let it go. Jesus forgave us, and we could do no less for those who had wronged us. I then explained that the foot-washing service was a time to wash these feelings away.

As I preached, I knew that I was not making it. The words were true, but they were just words to me. I felt miserable, wanting everything to work so well, but sensing no power in my preaching.

A baby cried. The mother cradled the infant in her arms and tenderly rocked him back and forth as she hurried down

MY FEET NEED WASHING, TOO

the side aisle. My heart wept as I wished for the comforting arms of the Father to be around me, loving me. But I had no such reassurance as I continued my sermon. Cutting things short, I directed the people to the various rooms for the foot-washing.

Then I washed my son's feet and everything changed. The problems of the day evaporated and I too, felt the power of the Holy Spirit at work on myself and upon my congregation.

The elder brought my wandering mind back to reality.

"You and your son have such a beautiful relationship," he smiled as he spoke. "Love just seemed to flow between you when you embraced after you washed each others' feet." He paused as if thinking back to those moments. "Thanks again for such a beautiful experience today."

I turned away so he would not see my eyelids blink as I tried in vain to hold back the tears. If he only knew! If the people only knew!

Two weeks ago yesterday, Tim had put a big dent in the fender of my car when he was turning it around in a parking lot. I almost never let him drive my car, and when I did, he wrecked it. The incident had left me extremely angry with him. For two weeks we both had avoided speaking to each other. Somehow, God got us together in the foot-washing service. While on my knees at his feet, the Lord spoke to me and I realized what the whole service was all about. My heart needed changing! I had to let go of my anger toward my own son. It was destroying our relationship and my relationship with Jesus.

Silently I prayed for help to release that anger. We finished washing each others' feet and stood facing each other. Suddenly the irritation vanished as I realized just how much I loved that boy.

"I'm sorry, son," I looked into the eyes of the almost adult

MY FEET NEED WASHING, TOO

teenager, "you're more important to me than any stupid old car. I love you, Tim."

We had just stood there staring at each other for what seemed like a long time. Breaking that moment, Tim replied, "I'm sorry, too, Dad, I . . ." He never finished that sentence; I wouldn't let him. Instead I hugged him.

My elder was right. The Holy Spirit had been laboring very hard that day. He worked on the pastor. Now you know why sometimes we ministers need to have our feet washed, too.

Watch Every Word You Say!

When a pastor moves to a new district, he often gets advice from the departing minister. In one church the new pastor may be urged to act conservatively. In his second congregation he could be warned against ever mentioning what is going on in the first one. For the third church a more liberal approach may be suggested. A pastor just beginning his ministry has a hard time remembering all the kindly advice the departing pastor gives.

I had such a problem in my first district. The former minister asked me to meet him at the post office of the largest of my three towns. Wanting to orient me to the churches, he felt that I would need extra help to get off to a good start.

The two of us spent an enjoyable morning visiting the members he liked. After lunch he introduced me to the second church and its problems. Strangely, we ran out of time before we could visit the third church, but he admitted as we separated that he had had problems with the congregation.

"You have a member there who used to be a Baptist minister," he grimaced as he spoke. "There are only 12 members, and everyone trusts him. . . . They listen to everything he says. If you make one mistake, he will stand right up and correct you in front of everyone!"

Now I grimaced.

"Whatever you do, don't antagonize him in any way! Watch every word you say!" Stopping the car, he pointed his finger at me. "The minister before me almost had a fist fight with him. This guy stood up during the sermon and corrected old Elder Trump. Trump got mad and told him to sit down, but the member wouldn't until the pastor apologized. It was a mess. A few weeks later they asked me to take over."

We sat in silence for a while. Here I was in my first district. How could I handle it? Even the seminary professors didn't stop me in the middle of a practice sermon. They always waited until I finished, and then let me have it.

"I'll be praying for you," he assured me.

It may have been all the people I had met that day. Or it may have been the result of a skipped meal. Whatever the reason, as soon as I saw him drive off, I realized that I had not written the man's name down. And I couldn't remember it!

During my first Sabbath morning in my first district a vision haunted me all day long. My imagination depicted me preaching away and then a strong, faceless voice challenges me from the congregation. My introduction sermon, my image as a minister, was shattered! All through the morning, I kept dreading the third congregation.

The members in my largest church appeared to accept me, and the people at the second one were so friendly that I almost forgot about the third congregation. As I hurriedly drove to the third church the horrible vision returned. Oh, how I wished I had written my antagonist's name down.

When I drove up, I saw several cars in the parking lot of the one-room white church. For a few minutes I sat in my Plymouth and tried to remember all the psychology classes I had slept through. But I knew psychology wouldn't work, so I prayed.

"O Lord, keep this man from destroying what You want me to do here today. Please take away my fear. Help me to be myself." God didn't take away my fear, however.

Someone heard my car door slam shut. The front door of the little church swung open, revealing only nine people, all of them staring at me. I knew that one of those nine had it out for ministers and was just waiting for me to flub up.

The elder, who had opened the door, shoved a large open

hand toward me, welcoming me to the church. I spoke as firmly as possible, trying to sound confident, and yet not offensive. Others swarmed to greet me, asking about my family and all the things they say to a new minister.

One man stood a distance away, avoiding eye contact, only coming up to shake my hand when I looked directly at him. Suddenly I knew! He must be the former Baptist minister.

Oh, how I prayed that afternoon. "Lord, help me not to blow it on my first Sabbath!"

The boisterous, smiling local elder called for the offering. My enemy came forward to take it up but he wouldn't glance at me. Becoming more nervous, I tried not to stare at him. Out of the corner of my eye I watched him return to his seat on the back row. Crossing his arms and leaning back, he gazed down at the floor. I knew he had to be criticizing every word I said.

But before I got to my second text, I realized that he was asleep! What a beautiful way to have a prayer answered, I thought. Relief flooded over me. Relaxed, I preached away —not very loud, however.

The next Sabbath afternoon found me fretting again. How would the Lord deliver me this time? The elder met me at the door and gave me a great welcome. Everyone else smiled—everyone but the deacon. He seemed to be watching me very carefully. I did the same to him.

This time I started the sermon very quietly, almost in a whisper. Before I completed the introduction and gave my first text, he again fell asleep.

It happened that way every week. As soon as I would start my sermon, he would go to sleep. As a result, I became braver and braver, venturing out into topics which were controversial at the time.

After a few more weeks, I screwed up my courage and visited in the home of the deacon. His wife seemed friendly as

WATCH EVERY WORD YOU SAY!

she offered to get me a glass of lemonade. Then she got up from the porch swing and left the deacon and me alone. I felt the tension in the air. He must have felt it as well. While he still wouldn't look me in the eye at first, as the visit went on, I discovered a very shy man. Should I really be afraid of this timid soul? Underneath this quiet exterior, however, there must be a real tiger. If he ever let go, I would be in trouble. My mother used to tell me, "Still water runs deep!"

My visits with the other members of that church were much more relaxed. The elder and I would sit back and argue over minute points of doctrine and church organization. He would get louder and so would I. But we joked with each other and had a great time. Without his help, I thought, this church would be in trouble. And without his support, I would be in trouble here.

During one of our visits I asked the elder about the deacon's background. "Where did Mr. Hill preach when he was a minister?"

"Mr. Hill?" He raised his eyebrows and thrust his face toward me. "He's never been a minister! Where in the world did you get that idea?"

"I heard from Elder Hofler before I moved here that he'd been one." Naturally I felt uneasy letting him know that the previous pastor and I had talked about the members.

"He wasn't any preacher, no matter what Elder Hofler says," the elder thundered as he shook his head vigorously. "Now me, that's another story. Back a few years ago, I attended the Baptist Seminary before I joined this church. I thought Hofler knew that."

Quickly finishing the conversation, I drove home. It became clear as I pulled into my driveway. For six months I had been afraid of the wrong man! If I had reacted the same way toward my elder, he wouldn't have trusted me either. From the first day we had mutual trust. Toward him and most of the others, I had been myself, preaching what I believed

MY FEET NEED WASHING, TOO

God wanted me to present. I made a vow that day that from then on, I would never discuss the church members with the departing pastor again. The mistakes I make with church members would be my own. I believe God has blessed that decision.

Poor Preaching

No minister deliberately wants to be a poor preacher. We study hard to master the techniques of sermonizing. It comes naturally to only a few. In college, however, a ministerial student receives many opportunities to learn to preach well.

I entered homiletics class my junior year hoping to become a master rhetorician. My instructor realized the impossibility of that vision. Before he even allowed any of us to practice preaching to each other, he insisted that we listen to some of the great preachers via the tape recorder. His second requirement included a personal appointment with him. During it he reviewed the outline for our sermons and offered suggestions for improvement.

As he looked at my outline he graciously smiled, then sighed deeply. After working it over, he sent me out to try to put "flesh on the bones" of my skeleton sermon. He wanted it to come alive.

Each student would preach to the rest of the class. We experts on pontification would sit with a piece of paper and pen in front of us. Then we took turns telling each speaker the things wrong with his sermon. I made the mistake of preaching only 21 minutes my first time. That left 34 minutes for the students to tell me what I had done wrong. They used up every available second!

The next time I took my outline into the private chambers of the master, I tried hard to listen to his remarks. Once more he pointed to the weaknesses of my outline. Once more I left the office with a red-marked-up piece of paper. And once more I carried the admonition to put some "flesh on the

MY FEET NEED WASHING, TOO

bones" of my sermon. Make it live, he had said. I sighed deeply.

With much fear, I stood before my peers when my turn came again. This time I preached thirty-five minutes. That left only twenty minutes for the criticism. They used it and half of the break between classes and were still going strong when the teacher mercifully told them to stop and let me go.

A third time I entered the office of the instructor. Again I handed him my outline and listened as closely as I could. There had to be something I was missing, something extremely important. As he tried to help me with the paper, he again suggested how I could improve the material. Then he gave me the same advice: "put flesh on the bones, make it come alive."

That night I studied his "improved" outline. It just wasn't me. Although I didn't tell the teacher, I threw his outline in the wastebasket and began a completely new one. This time I would preach my own sermon. And I couldn't wait to present it to those guys.

Eventually my turn came. With a strong feeling of righteous indignation I walked to the front of the class. They sat smugly at their posts, their pens poised, waiting for my first mistake. Having spent many hours studying Scripture and other outside sources, I knew my material. In addition, I had practiced out in the woods near my apartment. I was ready. Using the best delivery I could, I shared with those young men my words of wisdom.

After I finished, the silent class sat there for fifteen minutes before anyone spoke. You see, I had preached a strong sermon on criticism.

The teacher gave me an A+ on that attempt. From that day on I decided to preach sermons the way I felt the Lord wanted me to.

The seminary had a more subtle way of teaching ministers to preach. In those days they assigned a fledgling minister to a church nearby where he could practice before a real congregation.

At least these critics sat in front of me with their Bibles open, and I found them to be much more forgiving.

One week I chose sheep as a topic. Didn't the Bible say that "all we like sheep . . ." I read the *Seventh-day Adventist Bible Commentary* and tried to recall what others had said about sheep in our practice sermons while in college. Then I preached a beautiful discourse to a little church in the country. The "bones had flesh." I made those sheep walk around and "baa," and made them come alive to that congregation. They sat upright in the pews and watched me carefully. Never had an audience given me such rapt attention. I figured it must be the first time they had ever heard anything like this. When I finished, they all told me how interesting it was. But they said "interesting" in a funny way.

After church I received a dinner invitation. As we sat around the kitchen table at the farmhouse, I made simple conversation.

"What do you raise on this farm?"

The host choked on the juice he was drinking, then replied slowly, "We raise livestock."

"That's nice," I responded. I should have stopped but didn't. "What kind of livestock do you raise?"

"Sheep."

The rest of the meal was extremely quiet. Before I left, I asked them how accurate my discourse on sheep had been. They were kind.

"Our sheep have never acted like you said."

I thought it wise not to ask any more questions since they obviously didn't like having to give me the answers. The ride back to the seminary took a long time. I have never preached about sheep since. And I am sure those people would approve of that decision.

Several years and several churches later, after my first

sermon in a new congregation, Mrs. Burtch complimented me on her way out.

"I stayed awake today!" she smiled brightly. Before I could gain my composure to ask her what she meant, she left.

The next week she exited beaming and shook my hand vigorously. "This is two weeks in a row! I stayed awake today, too!"

"What do you mean, you stayed awake?" I asked her.

"I always sleep during the sermon, but you keep me awake. I have never stayed awake two weeks in a row."

It became a challenge. I would watch Mrs. Burtch. Whenever I saw her starting to doze, I knew I must be losing others as well. At that point, I would shout, speak softly, tell a joke, or quit preaching.

When guest speakers visited that church, I would sit where I could watch the woman. I still smile when I remember her coming through line after one guest speaker finished. She leaned over and whispered in my ear so he wouldn't hear. "I went to sleep today. He couldn't keep me awake."

Having been watching, I already knew. I had just observed my conference president putting her to sleep that morning.

In that same church a woman volunteered to be my secretary. Immediately I assigned her several duties. As we were discussing her tasks on Monday morning she confessed that she felt my sermons were improving—improving in relationship to her praying.

"When you and the elders walked onto the platform and knelt, I used to pray, 'Lord bless the lips that speak to us today.' As a result I began to appreciate your preaching more."

"Thank you." I felt good. But she continued.

"Then one morning, the Lord impressed me to pray a different prayer."

"What was that?"

POOR PREACHING

"Lord, bless the lips of he who speaks and the ears of those of us who hear." She sat in silence for a moment. "When I started praying that prayer, your sermons came alive and I have really been blessed."

I have never been accused of having a poor sermon by those who pray that prayer. When I sit and listen to another minister and pray the same way, I am always blessed.

Would You Visit My Father?

Have you ever wanted to go someplace and not have people recognize you? On one occasion I hoped no one there knew me as a minister for the Seventh-day Adventist Church.

During church one Sabbath morning I spotted two visitors sitting a third of the way from the back on my left. The man had graying hair and his face was quite pale. He did not have a tie on. His coat and trousers were at least one size too small and certainly not in current style.

A younger woman sat beside him, wearing more modern clothing. As I preached, she made eye contact and nodded her head in agreement at the right times.

The two visitors came through the line after the sermon. I asked them their names and where they were from. The young woman did the talking.

"This is my father, Bill Gardner, and my name is Barbara Johns. I'm visiting from out west, my father lives here...."

"Well, I'm glad to meet you, Barbara and Bill. How long will you be visiting here? Are you members of the Adventist church?"

"I'm a member back home." She stopped and we turned toward her father.

"I'm not a member now," he said softly. "I used to be a member in another place and time...."

"Well, you just feel free to worship with us, even if you are not a member," I urged.

In a few minutes the rest of the congregation had left the foyer. Going to the guest register, I looked up their names and found the address of Bill Gardner. Since I drove past his

WOULD YOU VISIT MY FATHER?

house every day on my way to the church, I told myself that I must visit him sometime.

The next week, Bill and his daughter were in their same seats. Once more Barbara followed the sermon, while Bill sat detached and apparently disinterested. After church they once more came through the line. Bill slipped past and quickly went out the door. Barbara paused and held onto my hand a little longer.

"Would you visit my father sometime? He could use some help. Thanks." She quickly left before I could ask her what kind of help he needed.

Several times I passed by his house but didn't stop. Later in the week I dropped by to make sure he felt welcome to return to church without his daughter. He wasn't home.

Bill did not come to church the next week, so I again tried to make contact. Once more no one answered my knock. I then began to look for a car in the drive. It never worked out. Every opportunity I had time to visit, there was no car in the drive. When I was late, a car would be sitting by the house.

Bill came to church only one more time. He sat in the usual place. At one point in my sermon, he appeared to be paying attention. During the closing song, however, he slipped out the door. I promised myself that I would visit him that week.

Again, it was a busy week. Again I found myself looking at the house as I sped by without time to stop. Other visits consumed my time and eventually I almost forgot about Bill Gardner and his daughter.

Reading the newspaper one day I noticed a familiar name. Bill Gardner had died. I read the story, and then reread the article again. A peculiar feeling crept over me as for a third time I went over the account of his death. What it didn't say particularly intrigued me. The report did not tell what he died of, or how he had died.

The next day the paper carried a follow-up article. Again,

it omitted any information about how he had died. But it did list the time and place for his funeral.

I canceled my appointments and went to the funeral. The casket was closed and the participants used words that would not have been employed at a Seventh-day Adventist service. The minister read the obituary and it seemed as if everyone there knew something I didn't know. It was not what was said that bothered me, but what was not. How had Mr. Bill Gardner died?

I sat in the back and left as soon as possible. While I didn't see the daughter there, I did recognize my barber who acted as a pallbearer.

As soon as I could I went to get my hair cut. Clearly I had never made a deep impression on him because every visit he would ask me again what I did for a living. As usual he did most of the talking. However, for a change he did not ask me where I worked, and I didn't volunteer to tell him. Finally, I got my nerve up and asked him about the funeral.

"You told me you were a member of the church down the street, didn't you?" I paused for his answer.

"Yeah, I've been a member there for years."

"I noticed that you had a funeral there last week." That was all I had to say. He took over and I got my facts.

Bill Gardner had been dying of cancer and suffering severe pain. Because the cancer had been discovered too late, he had had no hope. Bill had been attending that church for some time.

Apparently, I thought to myself, he did not feel comfortable enough to come back to a Seventh-day Adventist Church, or maybe the pastor hadn't made him feel welcome.

When Gardner got to the place that he knew that he would have to go to the hospital and would never come out, he couldn't take it. My barber told how the police at first had suspected foul play. He went on to describe in graphic detail how Bill had taken his shotgun into the bathroom to kill himself. On his first attempt, at the last second, Bill had evidently turned his head away. The blast had blown a large hole in the ceiling. With his second shot, he had killed himself.

It seemed like a year before the barber finished cutting my hair and I could get out into the fresh air. I found myself involuntarily shaking my head No as I started my car and drove away. I had failed.

A lot of things went through my mind that day. Should I give up being a minister? Although I had attempted to see him, he hadn't been home! I should have tried harder to make contact. Could God ever trust me again with suffering people?

The incident took place almost 18 years ago, and I still hurt. I know that God has forgiven me. Sometimes, when I feel tired and want to quit early, or I want to skip making some pressing visit, I remember Bill Gardner. I don't always know what is driving people, and until I do, I must find out what their problems are and how I can help them.

My prayer that day—and today—is, "May I never have to hope that people do not know that I am a Seventh-day Adventist minister."

A New Church:
The Pastor's Perspective

When a pastor moves to a new district it is a traumatic time for both him and the congregation. He wants to meet the needs of his new flock. For many years I used to think I knew what most of those expectations were before I ever started visiting.

For example, I assumed that they would expect me to treat everyone the same—the elderly, youth, old members, new members, and prospective members. They would want me to be consistent.

I did conclude correctly that the members of a rural community desired lots of visits in their homes. My problem was finding those homes.

On my first Sabbath, during the announcement time, I asked the congregation to tell me where they lived. In my attempt to be organized and consistent, they would have to help me. I informed them that I did not have a good memory. If they wanted a visit, they would need to draw me a map describing how to get to their home.

I knew that if everyone came up to me and said, "Look for the red barn on the way to the granary by the big pond," I would be lost. Especially if three or four of them gave me that kind of directions all at the same time.

"Please," I urged, "don't just tell me that you live three houses down on the left. Write it down on a piece of paper and then I will be sure to find you."

As I greeted the people on the way out of church, several of them handed me maps drawn on the inside of a tithe envelope torn open (back then the smaller churches did not have bulletins with blank pages on the back).

A NEW CHURCH: THE PASTOR'S PERSPECTIVE

One elderly woman approached me and began to give directions. "I live right down . . ." she began to point as I cut her off.

"Please," I interrupted her, "draw me a map and I will be sure to visit you very soon."

"But it's not that hard to find," she persisted, "it's just. . . ."

"I'm sorry," I replied. "If everyone gave me verbal directions, I would forget where they lived and would spend so much time looking that I wouldn't have time to visit. Thank you." I tried to be polite but yet firm.

She did not give me a map to her house, nor did I visit her, either. As I stopped by the homes of the other members in a regular fashion, we became acquainted and I discovered them to be lovely people. Since I had grown up in a rural community similar to theirs, the common background made it easy for us to accept each other. All except Mrs. Jacobs.

Although she never smiled at me, she also never brought up the subject of the map when we greeted each other before and after church—and I didn't either. I tried to be as kind as I could, but she still didn't accept me. I knew I had to visit her, but my pride and hers would not allow either of us to yield to the other.

In church one Sabbath I used an illustration that one of the farmers had given me. I told the congregation that Mr. Foster had shared the details of the story with me while we stood out by his barn. By that I wanted the people to know that they could influence me, that I would listen to them.

After church, Mrs. Jacobs studied me as she came to the door. After the usual greeting, she paused and looked me in the eye.

"You haven't visited me yet!"

I didn't respond, but smiled at her, thinking to myself, *she knows the rules—no map, no visit.* My heart, however, would not let this situation continue over something as stupid as a hand-written map on a piece of paper.

MY FEET NEED WASHING, TOO

Later in the week, during a visit with the Sabbath School superintendent, I asked for some help.

"Would you mind drawing me a map of how I can find Mrs. Jacobs' house?"

"Yes . . . I can if you want." She stared at me with a strange expression. "It's not that hard to find. . . ."

"I just want a map," I interrupted her.

"Do you want me to draw it from here, or where?" She tore a yellow piece of paper off the pad she had been taking notes on.

"From the church." I figured that would be easier for me.

She made a few marks on the paper and glanced at me with a quizzical look on her face. Not wanting to tell her about the running battle with Mrs. Jacobs, I smiled to myself that I would win the war without anyone else knowing there had even been a conflict. I figured that if she bragged about getting a visit without a map, my superintendent would tell others that she had drawn one for me.

"Do you want me to explain?" The tone of her voice surprised me.

"No, I'm sure I can figure it out."

"I'm sure you can, too." She folded the yellow sheet and handed it to me.

After I had driven a few miles I decided that today was the day I would visit Mrs. Jacobs. Stopping the car, I opened the map. Then I discovered that it certainly would be easy to find her home.

I did visit her that afternoon. She smiled at me for the first time when she saw me standing at her door.

Naturally I didn't explain to her that the superintendent had drawn me a map. And I hoped that the superintendent wouldn't tell her or anyone else either. The map was quite simple. It had a large box and a line which she had labeled "church and highway." Three other little

A NEW CHURCH: THE PASTOR'S PERSPECTIVE

boxes each represented a house. She used bold letters beneath one of those little boxes. It read "Mrs. Jacobs' house."

Mrs. Jacobs lived three houses down the street from the church.

A New Pastor:
The Members' Perspective

How do you relate to a new pastor? He assumes that you have questions about him, such as, How well does he preach? Will he visit? What things will he want to change? One of his biggest personal questions is, How well will he be accepted?

Some members will reveal this to him only slowly. Others will quickly let him know what they think. I have experienced both extremes when meeting my new church members.

Ralph, one of the elders of my new church, motioned for me to stop my car in the parking lot one afternoon. "Do you have a few minutes so we can talk?" he asked.

"Sure, get in." I opened the door to my car and he slid in on the passenger side.

"You are going to hear some things about me and the former pastor. I want you to get it straight from me."

"OK." I nodded for him to continue.

"Pastor Williams was here for five years. During that time, I did all that I could to help him be a success. To make a long story short, he just didn't make it! The church was dying. Members had quit coming. He wasn't visiting anyone. His sermons were shallow."

As I sat quietly, he looked at me. I again nodded for him to go on.

"He would find stories for the children just before we went onto the platform. He refused to work with me. Things were really bad. Something had to be done. I only did what I had to do."

Pausing, he waited for me to respond.

A NEW PASTOR: THE MEMBERS' PERSPECTIVE

"What did you do?"

"Haven't the others told you?"

"No." He was the first one to bring up the former pastor.

"Well, they will be telling you that I ran him out." Again he lapsed into silence. I had been concentrating, studying the car's dash. Then I slowly turned and looked at him. "I went to the conference office," he resumed, "and told them how bad a job he was doing and that we were in trouble here. They promised me that something would be done.... I am so happy that you are here. Even after a few weeks, I know that we will be having real church growth now. I just want you to know that I did what I had to do for the church. None of the others were willing to do anything, so . . . I did what was necessary. . . ."

Our conversation went on for a while longer. He told me that it was the hardest thing he had ever done, that the congregation felt bad that he had gone to the conference office and were angry with him for "running the pastor off." Concluding, he said, "Even if it becomes necessary, I have promised myself that I will never do it again. It just hurts too much. I am so happy you are here. I just know that things are going to be better."

Ralph had told me much more than he thought. Time would reveal if my first impression was right.

In another church Mrs. Moody reflected a different extreme. During my first visit to her home, she announced, "Pastor, I'm sorry, but I won't be able to work with you very much."

"Mrs. Moody," I was shocked, "several of the members have told me that you were very active with the program of the church. They told me that if there ever was anyone I could count on, it would be you. Have I done something wrong?"

"Oh, no! It's nothing like that," she blushed, "it's just . . . I was so close to the other pastor and his family. I loved his wife and children. When they left, it hurt so much."

"Oh, I see...." I didn't know what to say, so we just sat there for a moment.

"It just left a big empty feeling," she continued. "I hope you will understand. I would love to get better acquainted with your wife and children . . . but I just can't."

Tears filled her eyes. She also had told me much more than she realized. I left with a warm feeling in my heart. Time would tell if I was right or not.

Ralph had said that even if it became necessary, he would never go to the conference office about a pastor again. However, he couldn't keep that promise he had made with himself. This time, he had to let the office know of my shortcomings. Ironically, he used the same accusations that he had on the previous pastor: I didn't visit, members were no longer coming, the sermons were shallow, I had no organization, and I would not work with him to make things better.

In that small conference, I had been in the homes of nearly every one of those committee members to whom he had appealed. I had prayed in their homes. Most of them considered me their friend. And even before he got to them, I had already announced my move to a new conference. Attendance at church was better than it had been for a long time.

He would really have been surprised to know that the conference president and the conference committee members had urged me to stay in the conference. Those leaders had known as I did, that sooner or later Ralph would turn against me as he had every pastor before.

Mrs. Moody didn't keep her promise either. She came out of church one day and hugged me. The hug surprised me, but I was more pleased with what she said.

"I am so mad at you!" She held me at arm's length. "You have the nicest wife and kids. I even like you. I didn't think I could ever love a pastor like I loved Pastor Turner and his

A NEW PASTOR: THE MEMBERS' PERSPECTIVE

family. Now I've got attached to you and your family too. One of these days you will up and leave us and I will cry and hurt all over again!" Once more there were tears in her eyes, and mine as well.

Not everyone who dislikes the pastor will automatically dislike the new one. Nor will everyone who loves the previous pastor feel the same way toward the new one—but most do. What makes the difference? I don't know for sure. I do know that those who make a point of telling me how they feel before they even know me, reveal more about themselves than they think.

With few exceptions, those members who meet me and begin to tell how bad the man ahead of me was, will sooner or later turn on me. Those members who brag about the effectiveness and love of my predecessor will soon be giving me the same support and love as well.

Should I Try
to Get Him a Job?

"Pastor, I need to have the church pray for me," Frank told me over the phone one day.

"What's the problem?"

"Well," he began, "my boss tells me that unless I take my turn working on Saturdays, he is going to fire me."

"We surely will pray for you, Frank. As a matter of fact, I'll even go with you to talk with your boss if you want."

"No, don't do that. I just want the church to pray for me right now. I've got a little time before this becomes mandatory."

I assured him that I would have the church remember him in prayer. Frank and his wife Anita had become members of the church shortly before the conference assigned it to me. She had been a Christian in her youth, while he had not had much to do with anything religious before joining our church. The congregation did not know a lot about them either. We enjoyed watching them grow in their relationship with the Lord.

At prayer meeting we had special prayer for Frank and Anita. The members expressed real concern. During the church service the congregation remembered their needs.

Later the next week, Jack, my treasurer stopped by the church office. He brought up Frank's upcoming Sabbath problem.

"Pastor, I've been working at my job at the store for 25 years. They like me there."

"I'm not surprised, Jack," I told him. "You really care for anyone in need around here."

"Anyway, at work, a man is going to be fired. I know the

SHOULD I TRY TO GET HIM A JOB?

boss real well. I think I could get Frank a job there, and Sabbath would not be a problem."

"Hey, that's great! The Lord surely answers prayer." Then I realized that Jack wasn't smiling.

"There's a problem. . . ."

He went on to explain that a Seventh-day Adventist had worked at the plant before he did. The boss and the Adventist had not hit it off very well. The man had been a real righteousness-by-works kind of guy and would not allow anyone to differ with him without pounding him with texts. It had taken Jack years to win the boss over. They now had mutual respect for each other as Christians.

"So you see, if I recommend Frank and he doesn't work out, I will have ruined all I have tried to do for 25 years." We sat in silence for a bit. "What do you think I should do?"

Realizing we had a problem, we prayed and asked for wisdom. The Lord impressed both of us with an answer. If Frank was willing to put his faith on the line, even to the point of being fired for keeping the Sabbath, Jack would put his faith on the line and recommend Frank. It became my job to help build up Frank's faith without telling him that Jack might have employment for him.

Eager to visit with Frank again, I told him how I was sure the Lord would see him through his dilemma. The man sat grimly, listening to my encouragement without saying much. Finally, he spoke.

"Next week the boss says I work on Saturday or he fires me."

"What are you going to do, Frank?"

For a second he looked away and down to the floor. Then he took a deep breath and blew it out.

"I'm going to work. I have too many bills to pay. I just can't take a chance."

Oh, how I prayed for wisdom to know what to say next. I wanted to tell him about my conversation with Jack, how the church treasurer would put his reputation on the line if only Frank would follow what God had asked him to do.

"Frank, can I go with you to talk to your boss?"

"No, it wouldn't do any good."

"Frank," I pleaded, "I just know that God will not let you down. You must trust Him. He will never ask you to do anything He will not help you with."

I watched him tighten his jaw. He had made up his mind and nothing I could say would change him. The next Sabbath, Anita and the children were at church while he worked.

How many times has God answered my prayers and I never accepted that answer because of a lack of faith? Too many times, I'm sure.

"You Don't Know Me..."

Why does the telephone have to ring so late at night? I thought as I tried to force myself awake.

During my early years in the ministry, I would practice saying "hello" until I convinced myself that I was in fact awake. Now such a procedure isn't necessary. I have learned to wake up all at once. Going back to sleep continues to be a problem, however.

"Hello," I tried to sound fully awake, failing.

Silence greeted me. Listening without saying anything for a second, I prepared to hang up the receiver. Then I heard a coin clink. My late night caller was using a pay phone that required a coin after the other party made connection. Before anyone spoke I heard the sound of country music blaring through the line.

"Hello," I repeated.

"Is this the pastor?" a heavily slurred voice made me wince. Another drunk.

"Yes, this is the pastor. What can I do for you?"

"My name is Glenn Scott . . . you don't know me, but . . ." He went on talking but my sleepy mind wandered.

I did know Glenn Scott. At least I did by reputation. He had made nearly every member in his small church extremely agitated. Ever since I had arrived, they had been after me to visit him. They wanted action, now!

The man had been arrested for public drunkenness so many times that it had greatly embarrassed the congregation. Wanting him disfellowshipped, they told me of the many times the newspaper would report that he had been arrested for this or that. I promised them I would take care of the problem in time.

Now I forced myself to listen to the voice on the telephone.

"I need help." He lapsed into silence and the noise of the bar came clearly through the receiver.

"What kind of help do you want from me?"

I knew what to expect. Such late night callers want to be taken home, they want more money for drink, they want someone to listen to them, they want to be rid of their guilt, they want someone to take the hurt away.

Why can't they call me when they are sober? I had spent many hours in my early ministry listening to a drunk tell me all the reasons why he drank. A sober wife asked me why I bothered to listen. "He won't remember a word you say," she had told me.

I had an answer in my innocence. "He will remember that I was here."

And he did—he was ashamed of himself and wouldn't talk to me about his situation while sober. The man knew that I had never taken a drink in my life and could not see how I could help him. When he remained sober, he didn't need a pastor's help.

Shaking my head once more to wake up, I listened to Glenn's request for aid.

"I don't know why I drink. . . . I want to quit. I know that you can help me, will you?"

Why do they think I can help? Even the wives and relatives assume I have all the answers to such situations. I am only human. All I can do is try. Even when I appeared to have success, I failed in their eyes. In that few seconds that Glenn talked I remembered trying to help the Molly family . . .

Fred Molly had led a rough life before that night he drove his car into the bridge abutment. The blood alcohol content level reached .19 according to the police report.

I had visited the family to offer my condolences. They were beside themselves with grief. His brother-in-law, Donald, had started drinking again, after two years of staying sober. Fred's wife and sister had begged me to make him stop. They kept telling me how mean he got when drunk.

"We just can't have him go to the funeral drunk. We have enough problems. Can you do something, anything . . . ?"

I had gone into the backyard where Donald sat holding his fifth of whiskey. He had held it up to me, offering me a drink. I shook my head and began to talk to him. We spoke about Fred and his life, about the funeral that Donald had to attend. Screwing up my courage, I prayed for extra help, then asked the man for something that I knew would be next to impossible.

"Donald, do you want to be drunk for the funeral? You know that you will not remember much of it if you are. You know how Fred died. Why not sober up at least for the funeral?"

So far I had gotten little positive response. We had talked about many things in that backyard that morning. But I had sensed that he was softening and pressed on in my requests.

"Donald, why not give me the bottle, please, for your family's sake?" I prayed and held my breath.

"What will you do with it, drink it yourself?"

"No, I'll do whatever you want me to do with it."

"Will you give it back to me after the funeral?" He turned his head and looked me in the eye.

What could I say? They had asked me to keep Donald sober for the funeral, to do anything I could to help.

"If you give me the bottle, I'll give it back after the funeral. I promise on my word as a minister." I had held out my hand to receive it from him.

It took a lot more than that, but in the end I left the

backyard with a two-thirds full bottle of whiskey in my coat pocket. Then I had gone into the house and told them that Donald would be sober. I had also explained that when the funeral was over the next day, I would return and try to talk Donald into letting me destroy the bottle. At that moment they had thought I could do anything. I couldn't.

The next afternoon I had met Donald in his yard again. This time a sober man talked to me. He had remembered our conversation and my promise and wanted the bottle back. I prayed and talked and begged but ended up giving it to him. The wife and sister have never forgiven me. They had wanted the impossible, they wanted me to change a man. I don't have that power. Only God does.

The telephone voice stopped and the country music filled the silence again. Glenn waited for me to say something. I snapped awake again.

"Glenn, did you drive to the bar tonight?"

"No," he slurred, "I came in a cab."

"If you want help, I want you to take a cab home right now." I paused, then asked, "Do you have any money left for a cab?"

"Yes."

"OK, listen to me, you take a cab home now, and tomorrow I'll come to your house. Where do you live now?"

Glenn told me his address. I knew the location. He at least was sober enough to get home for the rest of the night.

"I want you to call a cab and go home now, OK?" I repeated and waited for a response.

"OK." He said no more.

"I will visit you later in the afternoon tomorrow."

"I won't feel too good tomorrow." He must have just realized what I was going to do. "Can you come the next day?"

"If you want my help, Glenn, you go home right now. I am stopping by your house tomorrow! You call that cab right

"YOU DON'T KNOW ME..."

now. OK?" I pressed, hoping that I would not make him angry.

Before we hung up, I prayed with Glenn, asking for God to help him get control of his life. We went through the verbal exchange of having him call a cab a few more times. Then the phone went dead in my hand. My mind now became clear. How would this one turn out? I slept little the rest of that night.

The next afternoon I stood at the unpainted front door of Glenn's house, trying to recall every bit of reading I had done about dealing with alcoholics. Some would remember things said while they were drunk, others couldn't remember that they had even talked with anyone. How would Glenn react? I knocked on the door.

A very timid and short man opened the door just wide enough to look out. He obviously didn't feel too well. His red-glazed eyes and unshaven wrinkled face told a sad story.

"I'm the pastor you called last night. May I come in?"

He lowered his head, pulled the door open the rest of the way, and pointed to a dirty couch just inside. Sitting down, we began to talk.

Glenn Scott wanted to begin his life again. He and I discussed many things that afternoon. We spoke about his relationship with the church, about his need to start all over again. Then we explored how he should again have fellowship with Christians. Finally we talked about how only God could help him.

Several visits later, I brought a letter from Glenn Scott to the church board. In it he asked to have his name dropped from the membership of the Seventh-day Adventist church. He wanted to start with a clean sheet, to begin his life all over again. Glenn told them how he was now taking Bible studies with the pastor and hoped someday to be rebaptized. A week later the church in business session took action and removed his name from the church records at his request.

MY FEET NEED WASHING, TOO

It was fun to watch the first time Glenn Scott came back to church. He had shaved, showered, and had on clean clothes. The members did not know him.

God and I did.

Have You Ever Played Ping-Pong?

I finished the first lesson of the old "20th Century Bible" course with Jim. The study had not gone well. The noisy projector and the sheet thumbtacked to the wall as a screen seemed rather unprofessional. As I stood by the door with my slide projector and Bible getting ready to put my coat on, Jim spoke up on his own for the first time that night.

"Have you ever played ping-pong?"

"I'm not too good, but my brother had a table once," I replied.

"I have a table upstairs. Would you like to play a game sometime?"

"Sure, how about now?"

Sandra had a very puzzled look on her face as I laid my Bible down on the slide projector and went up the stairs with him. Belonging to one of the churches I pastored, she had asked me to give her husband Bible studies. I agreed to work with him if he wanted me to. When she had asked her husband if it would be all right for me to come by and study with them, he allowed her to make an appointment with me.

He had been raised as a Seventh-day Adventist but left the church when he became old enough to make his own decisions. Now he attended only when his children did something for Sabbath School. His wife and two little girls never missed services. Jim's mother had won Sandra to the Lord and now Sandra wanted her husband to join her.

As we studied that night, I hadn't felt like I was getting through to him. Jim remained quiet, never speaking unless directly addressed. Even then, he said as little as possible. It became evident to me that once again a family member expected the minister to do the impossible: "Win my loved one to the Lord for me because I can't." The longer we went that night, the more I wanted to get through that study. I had been at the door when he talked about playing ping-pong.

The old table leaned slightly to one side. The green paint was chipped and faded. Jim seemed a little more open as he volleyed for the serve. I won the serve, but never got a point during my first five tries. It was his turn. Grasping the paddle and starting to serve, he suddenly paused and spoke.

"I can't get baptized. I smoke."

He served and made another point. When he picked up the ball from the floor, I said, "Do you think it's wrong to smoke?" He served and I got the point. We continued to play and talked during the breaks.

"My mom and wife tell me that it is."

"But what do you think?"

"I remember studying about it years ago, but I don't know now. It's been so long."

"Tell you what, Jim, don't worry about smoking until you are convinced yourself that it is wrong. When the Lord tells you to quit, you will be clear on the subject."

"How will I know when that will be?" he asked when his turn to play came again.

"I can't answer that, but I'll tell you this, one of these days the Lord will say, 'Jim, it's time to stop smoking.' When that day arrives, you'll know. And with His help, you'll be able to quit. If the Lord can't convince you, don't worry about what your mother and wife say."

Jim beat me every game that night. I never even came close. During those 45 minutes we did more talking than during the entire Bible study. The look on Sandra's face when I came down those stairs told me that she didn't know what to think of her minister playing ping-pong with her husband when he came for a Bible study.

A week later I returned with the second lesson. Once

more we went through a Bible study. Sandra knew all the answers. Jim had not changed. He answered only when spoken to. As I stood by the door ready to leave, he again asked me if I wanted to play some ping-pong.

We were in the middle of the first game when Jim brought up religion.

"I have quit drinking."

"That's good. When?" I tried not to be too excited.

"Last week. The girls have been after me for a long time. I poured a six-pack down the kitchen sink. I still can't quit smoking, though."

Week after week I studied with the couple. Week after week he and I spent time alone in the game room above their living room. Jim opened up more and more and began to attend church more regularly.

Sandra and I prayed that the Lord would convict him. I watched as he gave his heart to the Lord. He became more and more convinced that he had to stop smoking, but just didn't feel like the Lord had told him to yet. By now I began to worry that maybe I had been wrong to speak so strongly about waiting until the Lord announced for him to stop.

The conference moved me to a new district. The pastor that followed me kept studying with him. Late one night, Jim and Sandra called me at my new home.

"You'll never guess what happened," Sandra practically yelled into the phone and then paused.

"What happened?" I yelled back.

They told me the story. Jim had been on the roof of a house under construction. As he leaned over to do some work, his cigarettes fell out of his pocket and slid down the roof. Going to the edge, he looked down to where he could see them lying in a ditch. When he started for the ladder to retrieve them, the Lord impressed him to leave them alone.

"It's just like the Lord told me, 'now is the time!' I think I can quit now."

Jim did. A short time later he was baptized into the Seventh-day Adventist Church. I never did beat him playing ping-pong. I guess I didn't need to.

Ingathering:
For Better or Worse

I think of Ingathering the same way I do of oatmeal. The bran in oatmeal has been proven to lower one's cholesterol. It is filled with other nutrients and vitamins one needs and is a good food for cold winter mornings. The problem is, I don't like oatmeal.

Ingathering is good for the church. The program gives the local congregation an opportunity to contact each of the people in the community and tell them about the church. It provides the local and world organization more funds to continue its operations of community good. Most importantly, it leads to individuals being won to God's kingdom. The problem is, I don't like Ingathering.

I do Ingathering because I believe it should be done. And I eat oatmeal because I love my wife and she wants me to stay around a little longer. To get the oatmeal down, I put in lots of dates, raisins, nuts, and other good things (sugar mostly, if she is not looking).

There are good things to put into Ingathering to help it go a little easier. You have to look for them though.

Weather keeps many people from Ingathering. Once my senior pastor encouraged the members to come out one Saturday night. He told us that the Conference Lay Activities leader would also be there that night. I expected a large group to participate but it rained that afternoon and evening. As a result only four people showed up. A driver, the conference man, the senior pastor, and the intern, me. We went Ingathering.

Many times I have suggested to church members that we go before the bad weather sets in. They reply, "We need to get into the Christmas spirit before we can go Ingathering."

Another fear people use to not participate is dogs. You stand at the gate and read and re-read the sign that says, "Beware of Dog." Do you go into the enclosure or do you walk by, rationalizing that no one would be home anyway? At another house, after you ring the doorbell, the inside of the house erupts with the sound of three thousand pounds of dogs all barking and jumping at the door. A little tiny woman answers and you try to tell her what you are doing there. At the same time you watch her try to keep the huge dogs from going through the thin screen door. It's hard to be heard above the noise of your knees knocking and the can rattling in your shaking hand.

Even the little dogs can get you. One night, John, one of my members, stood on the porch waiting for the woman of the house to return with an offering. His good friend Pat, walked by just as the family's little dog came around the house and up the steps of the porch. Knowing John's fear of dogs, Pat whispered just loud enough for him and the dog to hear, "Bite him!" The dog did. It was some time before John would talk to Pat.

The victory banquet is the best way to end an Ingathering campaign. In years past, the conferences used to have the ministers bring in the final totals and we would have a great banquet to celebrate our victory. My first such banquet came right after I finished the seminary and had been assigned to assist in a large church. We got only half our goal that year (see above, the conference Lay Activities Leader is coming). The banquet was held on Superbowl Sunday at the conference office. The senior pastor told me what time he would pick me up. I tried to tell him that I didn't need to go, but when he said that he wasn't going to face the music alone, and did I like washing cars for a living? I agreed to go with him.

At the appropriate time each pastor would stand during

the banquet and give the final Ingathering totals for his church. Some gave speeches, telling how certain individuals had really helped. Our turn came. The senior pastor stood. I tried to sit and slide under the table. His strong hand reached out and took me by the shoulder and practically pulled me to my feet. He spoke for two hours and fifteen minutes (at least it seemed like it) before he revealed our total. The term victory banquet didn't mean that much to me that day.

There are lots of ways to get out of door-to-door solicitation and still be involved with Ingathering. Some of them are better than others. Taking care of the kids who are too little to go out sounds like a good way to spend the evening as opposed to walking the streets. Wrong. Their parents know what they are doing. They are getting away from those kids for awhile. The first half hour you can sing songs. The second half hour you can play games. The third half hour you spend trying to get diapers changed. The fourth half hour crawls by as you try to get all of them to stop crying for their mothers. I think baby sitters have even been known to pray for some parents to quit and come in early.

Another way to be involved and not have to work so hard is to drive. A driver must keep track of where solicitors are and bolster their courage. He or she must have extra papers to restock them. The driver must insure that the car stays extra warm to help the cold church member. He must remember what streets have been worked and by whom. The driver must always have a smile on his face and motivate the lazy workers until they have covered their territory. Everyone wants to be a driver, even some who do not have cars.

One fear that many of us have, is that everyone will beat our total for the night. People expect the minister to do extra well. I came up with a plan that—when carried out—seems to help. I suggest that each of us pool our money. We try to reach a church goal instead of individual goals. Those who want to keep track of their own total do so themselves. We then do not quit until the church reaches its complete goal. Those who do well, keep on doing well, while those of us who do poorly, keep on trying. One particular night I knew that I had fallen into the latter category. When we got to the church and everyone was counting his money, I kept reminding them that we were trying to reach a church goal. Walking over to a table where the people in my car were counting their money, I dropped mine onto the pile in front of one of the solicitors. He could not tell how much was his and how much was mine. But I knew. All he had to do was subtract $1.47 from the total, because that was all that I had raised that night.

One of my little churches grew discouraged because they couldn't raise their church goal. I encouraged the other two churches which had reached theirs to spend one Saturday night helping their sister church. Calling the conference office, I asked for assistance from them as well. Two men arrived to help us. Neither of them felt any better about Ingathering than I did. They had managed all year to have other appointments which kept them from even helping in their own congregations.

We arrived at the church and were trying to get organized. A lay member who knew most of the people took over, paired the conference officers up with separate groups, and sent them out. Several times she looked at me, then changed her mind. Finally only one group remained. We went for the evening together. The last group out, we were the first back.

The conference men dragged in later. They had ridden with drivers who believed in staying out a long time. Those men were very happy to be back that night. The little church was also happy that night as well. For the first time in years they had reached their church goal. I was the happiest, however. Earlier in the evening when we had headed for the car, my lay activities leader had stopped me just before we got in.

INGATHERING: FOR BETTER OR WORSE

"I don't know how much Ingathering these men from the office have done this year, but I do know how much you have done. You drive tonight!"

I am still smiling because I never told my two good friends from the conference office that I drove that night while they trudged door to door through the snow.

Memories like these are the ingredients I use to sweeten Ingathering and make it go much better.

Don't Have Anything More to Do With Our Kids

I made a big mistake. Two children did not get to go on a Pathfinder campout who should have gone because I changed the rules in the middle of the contest. The children were upset and so were the parents.

Ingathering that year had not gone well. To make things more interesting, I promised every one of our youth that if they went out at least six times, I would take them on a campout. In January, when the Ingathering campaign finished, the weather turned bad and we could not go as I had planned. I forgot about the promise, thinking I would take them in the spring.

In February we started a Pathfinder Club. It consisted of the same young people who had helped me with Ingathering. We had a good time organizing. It started out strongly, but as we tried to prepare for the approaching Pathfinder fair, the enthusiasm waned somewhat. The Wilson boys did not show up as regularly as the others. We knew we had to put some kind of teeth in our attendance requirements.

When we talked it over as a club, someone reminded me that I had promised these same kids a campout. Why not have campout for the Pathfinders and say that if anyone did not come to a required number of meetings, they would not be eligible to go on it that spring? It sounded good to me so we adopted the new rule.

It worked at first. The attendance picked up and we had everyone coming for awhile, then it slipped back to just a few. Eventually we set a date for the campout in May. Another Pathfinder club invited us to join them for an early spring outing 150 miles away. My wife would drive one car,

DON'T HAVE ANYTHING MORE TO DO WITH OUR KIDS

and I another. That limited us to only ten young people. We made it clear that to go, a camper would need to attend all of the remaining meetings prior to the campout. The Wilson boys missed several meetings without a good excuse.

Our campout was a beautiful success and we had a wonderful time. The weather turned out extremely warm for that time of year and the food was delicious. My club enjoyed the exposure to a group of Seventh-day Adventist young people from a distant town. Sunday night arrived too soon for all of us. The parents laughed as the tired group of campers tried to separate their sleeping bags and gear from all the others.

At church the next week I noticed a coldness from the Wilsons. They knew the rules, I thought to myself. You come to the meetings or you do not get to go camping. After the sermon, one of the young people who had gone on the campout told me that the Wilsons were extremely upset at me. I already knew that, but if the problem was being talked about behind my back, I would have to take care of it.

I telephoned the parents and asked for an appointment one evening that next week. My wife and I drove to their country farm home. It was a warm spring day. The fresh fragrant smells wafted through the open windows as we motored along. I could talk my way out of any problem—or so I thought. And besides, the situation was not major anyway.

A confident pastor walked up the steps of the porch. We did not have to knock on the door because the family had already assembled to wait for us. My wife and I took seats on the couch. The boys sat near the door to the kitchen. The mother took a position across from us in an overstuffed chair. They were pleasant, but not happy. Suddenly I realized that it might be harder to resolve than I had at first assumed.

"I know that there has been a misunderstanding about the campout we just had," I began, "and I want to get it cleared up."

MY FEET NEED WASHING, TOO

Then I paused to watch for Mrs. Wilson's reaction. She showed none.

"For a camper to be able to go on the campout, it was required that they attend the meetings just before the campout. Your boys missed those meetings and were not eligible to go."

I tried to sound authoritative and yet kind. The woman did not change her facial expression but did begin to speak slowly.

"Didn't you promise these boys that they could go on a campout if they helped with Ingathering at least six times?" She paused until I answered.

"Yes, but . . ."

"They both went Ingathering seven times!"

A quick glance at her sons revealed pained expressions on their faces. Somehow I couldn't look Mrs. Wilson in the eye. Once more I tried to explain.

"We started the Pathfinders after Ingathering. The kids all voted to make the one campout do for both activities. I assumed that your boys were in agreement with that vote."

"That doesn't matter. You promised them a campout for Ingathering, and you did not keep your promise."

She had not raised her voice. The words were slow and firm. And Mrs. Wilson was right. I had not kept my word. We sat in silence for a few minutes while I thought. After an inaudible prayer, I began again.

"There's nothing I can say now, except that I am sorry. I hadn't thought about things that way. What can I do to make this thing right between us?"

When I glanced at the boys, they turned toward their mother. I faced her, too.

"There is nothing you can do. The damage has been done and . . ."

"Look," I quickly broke into the middle of her sentence, "maybe I can take these guys on a special campout, just the

DON'T HAVE ANYTHING MORE TO DO WITH OUR KIDS

three of us. I could take them to the museum down at the . . ." She didn't let me finish.

"No!" This time she raised her voice. "Don't ever have anything more to do with my boys again. There is nothing you can do!"

The raised voice and the tone she used let me know that this country mother had enough of me. My wife and I had to leave. I could think of no graceful way out.

"If you ever change your mind, let me know. I really am sorry. I . . ." The words were quiet and heartfelt.

Getting up from the couch, we started for the door. Mrs. Wilson had regained her composure as well. It seemed odd in light of everything else, but she called a greeting as we walked toward the car.

"We'll see you in church this weekend."

Somehow I managed to drive a mile from their home before I broke down and wept like a baby. My wife held me and I hugged back. I had blown it and would never be allowed to make it up to those boys. Yet I had been doing the best I could. It was an honest mistake.

Conditions were not the same in church after that evening. The Wilson boys still laughed at my attempts at humor during our lesson study, but the uneasiness remained. The Pathfinder club continued. In spite of the success in the district, I couldn't forget about the Wilson boys, yet there was nothing I could do. All I could think of I tried. In Sabbath School I gave them every bit of extra attention I could. Mrs. Wilson did not soften.

Within the year I moved from that district and started out fresh with a new group. Now I watch myself when I make promises to young people—and adults as well. I do still forget, but not like I did that time.

Fifteen years went by. Late one evening I received a phone call from the youngest Wilson boy. His brother had just been killed in an accident at the factory where he worked. The family wanted to know if I would have the funeral.

I drove many miles to get back to my old district, reaching it an hour and a half before the funeral. The family appeared grateful to see me. We hugged and talked of the boy. Mrs. Wilson related how he felt closer to me than any other minister they had ever had. I saw a lot of hurt in her eyes. After the service they thanked me for coming.

Once more, as I drove away from an encounter with the Wilsons, I cried again. Neither Mrs. Wilson nor I had brought up the last meeting that we had had. She didn't have to. The woman had finally accepted my apology, had at last forgiven me.

I still question myself, "Why did her son have to die before she could forgive me?" But there is no answer.

Moving Day

"I'm sorry," Dr. Saunders told me, "but we will not be joining the church here."

My personal ministry leader had found out by accident that Dr. Saunders would be taking over the Emergency Room at the local hospital. As a professional, he could bring life to the struggling church in the little town. Like many small churches, it had few men.

"It's a very friendly little church," I tried to sound encouraging without being pushy.

"Oh, I'm sure it is. But we have many friends in our home congregation, so we will be keeping our membership where it is. We will drive there each week."

The Saunders had not moved their family belongings to their new home yet. He and his wife were staying in an efficiency apartment until the closing on the new house. When Sabbath came, they would drive the 60 miles to their home church. They had not even visited my congregation. Something had to be done. I would do what was necessary.

Without being too obvious, I made several phone calls and found out when they would be moving. The conference moving van would load them in the morning, drive to our city, and unload them the same day. It would be a long day for them.

I decided that I would become a moving van assistant though it would be a long day for me too. When the van came through town on the way to pick up the Saunders family, the driver stopped to get me first. A most surprised doctor opened the door when we arrived.

"Where do I begin?" I asked. He stood there with his

MY FEET NEED WASHING, TOO

mouth open and then pointed to some boxes on the living room floor.

"Right there, I guess."

It was a long morning. We carried boxes and lugged furniture. And we laughed together when Mrs. Saunders handed me a garbage bag of trash, and started to throw away a box of clothes. By noon we had everything loaded. Two hours later the van pulled up in front of their new home.

Two men from our church arrived unannounced and asked if they could help. Once more, Dr. Saunders didn't know what to say.

It was a long afternoon. At six o'clock we were almost finished. A car drove up and parked by the street. Three of the women of the church had arrived. I watched and listened through an open window as they introduced themselves to Mrs. Saunders.

"Hi, we're from the church and heard that you would be moving here today. We just wanted to welcome you," my personal ministries leader held out her hand.

"Thank you," the physician's wife shook hands with the others as they introduced themselves. "I guess you know things are a mess, but if you want to see the house, come on in and I'll show it to you."

"We didn't come to do that," one of them quickly shook her head. "We brought you folk supper. Where do you want it?"

In a short time they had a picnic meal spread out on the cluttered living room floor. Thinking it best to leave before Dr. Saunders could ask me any questions, I didn't stay for supper.

Within a month the conference moved me to another district. At a constituency meeting later that year, I saw some of the leaders from my previous church. As we were greeting each other I noticed Dr. Saunders sitting in their section.

"Hello," I stepped over and shook his hand. "It's good to

see you here." Then I quickly walked away before he could talk to me.

Later I found out that Dr. and Mrs. Saunders were very involved with the little church. He had become the head elder and the representative from the church on the district school board. She had become a Sabbath School superintendent.

They may have been running, but they couldn't hide from the love of God's people in that little church. I have never told him how hard it was to get everything organized for that day. But it paid off for that little church and for Dr. and Mrs. Saunders.

The Affair

Elder Johnson, a guest speaker from the conference office, kept apologizing for having an altar call in one of my churches.

"I'm really sorry," he began after we walked down from the platform. "I felt like the Lord was telling me to have one. I tried to ignore the feeling, but it just wouldn't go away."

"Don't worry about it," I replied. "There was a reason." However, I was not at liberty to tell him what it was.

When a visiting preacher plans an altar call, he usually lets the home pastor know. The pastor knows who to pray for during the sermon while the guest preaches. The two can then become a team as one speaks and the other prays. Elder Johnson felt like he had violated that unspoken rule, and he was sorry. I was not.

A number of people in the congregation needed to make a decision to follow the Lord. Then the experience of letting others know of that decision, will bring about a response that strengthens everyone involved. It's sad that some become upset when a speaker makes such a call.

Jim Davis and I were working on a health fair booth at a local county fair. He had become the president of his own company, a small manufacturing concern. We had a good time the first day we manned the booth together. Near the end of our shift a young woman came by and struck up a conversation with Jim. I didn't think much about it until she started to leave.

"I'll see you tomorrow," she called out and left with her friends.

"Who was she?" I asked.

THE AFFAIR

"Oh, that's Sally, she works in shipping at the factory." He didn't say any more and we dropped the subject.

The next evening we took our shift again together at the fair. Jim kept looking at his watch, as if willing time to pass. Eventually Sally appeared and once more started talking to him. He spoke softly and laughed loudly. After a while she left with her friends. A few minutes later Jim told me he would be right back, then vanished for about 20 minutes in the same direction they had gone.

When he returned, he acted differently. I said a silent prayer and asked him once more about the young woman. He grew hostile at my question. Finally I got blunt and told him how it appeared.

"Jim, we've been friends a long time. I'm thinking of your best interests. There may be nothing going on, but this does not look good. You act differently around her. Is there anything going on?"

"You dirty-minded preacher," he spat out the words. "There is nothing going on here except in your mind. Just lay off will you?"

"I'm sorry if I offended you. I was just trying to help . . ."

"You close up, I'm through tonight." He quickly left.

Had I done the right thing? Jim was a local elder of the church. Was it proper for the pastor to question his morality? Had I made an enemy in the congregation? Only time would tell.

Jim began to behave differently on the church board as well. He grew extremely impatient when we dealt with a couple who were going through a divorce. I watched and listened to his comments which were laced with criticism of the couple.

At a church potluck he and his wife Linda went through the line together with their girls. Trying to balance three plates, Linda asked him for some help, only to have him explode in anger at her incompetence. Then he quickly apologized and tried to assist her.

When he had the morning prayer one Sabbath, I felt impressed that things were not getting better between him and his wife. The words of the prayer were repeats of his last time on the platform.

That week he asked me to go golfing with him and two of his employees. We had a great time. During the break after shooting nine holes, I went to get a soft drink. When I returned, I overheard one of the men teasing Jim about something. The man used the name Sally. Everyone laughed. When Jim saw me, he motioned for the men to stop and they did. But my mind didn't.

Later in the afternoon, Jim and I were waiting for the others. Once more I prayed before I spoke.

"Jim, if you need to talk to me about anything, remember that I care. Call me anytime." I didn't say anymore and he didn't reply.

At 12:30 in the morning a few days later my phone rang. It was Jim.

"Pastor, I'm in trouble. I have been having an affair. I need help."

We spent a long time on the phone that night, a long time counseling together, a long time praying together. Jim and Linda went for professional counseling and things really improved between them.

I never forced him to confess his sin to the church. It had not been common knowledge among the congregation. He had confessed it to God and to his wife, however, and they had worked things out.

Jim remained an elder. But now his prayers were different. A genuine smile had returned to his face. The whole congregation sensed the transformation.

Elder Johnson wondered why the Lord asked him to have the altar call that morning. I knew.

The first one to get to his feet and come down the aisle

THE AFFAIR

that morning was Jim Davis. Quickly I left my place on the platform and went down to meet him. Soon Linda and many others joined us in front of the church. No one in the congregation was surprised that a local elder would respond to an altar call.

No one but Jim, Linda, God, and I knew that he needed to.

The Beautiful Music

The music was as professional as any the church had ever heard. The pianist played without looking at either the keys or the music, her face aglow.

The soloist sang softly with great feeling, perfectly in time with the piano. She never glanced at her music which lay on the podium in front of her. Sitting on the side, I watched them perform. Sue's eyes sparkled in the soft light of the church. Several in the congregation were blinking hard. I couldn't see Sharon's eyes until she turned to walk off the platform, but then I knew she would need the handkerchief she carried in her hand.

It was the first time the two had performed together.

Sue lived in the same small town and had become a member after a hard struggle. Her musical talents at first kept her from joining with our small group of believers. The high school where she taught music needed her on Saturdays. The plays, the dances, the homecomings, the basketball games, and so many other activities took precedence over her religious life. She lived by herself with her birds. Even amid all the activities, she was a lonely young woman.

Children won her to the Lord. During a piano lesson, a young member of my church started talking to Sue about his church. The boy told her about our Sabbath School and the songs he knew and wanted to learn to play. He described the enjoyable things the church did together and how much fun the potlucks were. Jimmy invited her to come to church with him the next week.

As Sue sat near the front with the boy, I watched as she sang with gusto. I smiled to myself as she kept time with the

THE BEAUTIFUL MUSIC

organists' offertory by tilting her head back and forth. Within a short time everyone in the church loved Sue.

When Sue missed church because the band was marching in a parade on Saturday morning, the church did not condemn her, but kept holding out its hand and heart. After a year of attending and many Bible studies, she was buried in baptism in a beautiful service in the little church.

The young woman became the pianist right away and really livened up the place with the young sounds she loved. The organist had to learn new pieces of music so the two could play together. The little congregation really rocked when Sue led the song service. Everyone who had special music begged her to play for them. A professional, she never refused anyone. The young woman had found a family in the small congregation.

Sharon and her husband moved into the community after that. He had transferred from the west coast to manage the largest store in town. I sat behind her during Sabbath School the first day they attended church. Her beautiful soprano voice filled the sanctuary. Along with others near her, I stopped singing and listened to her as she sang the familiar hymn.

After church several people approached the organist—who arranged for all special music—and suggested that Sharon be asked to sing for church the next Sabbath. Sharon agreed. When they told her that Sue would play for her, she said that it would not be necessary.

I introduced her when her time to sing came the next week. She walked to the piano, sat down, and began to play. I saw no music, but heard her clear voice burst out with song. Even without a microphone, we could understand every word, every syllable. Sharon could sing and play beautifully.

After church many of the members rushed to thank her for her special music. At first just a few people who did special music had her play for them, but then more and more Sharon received requests to help and Sue less and less. Sue felt like she was losing her family.

Everything came to a head when the high school offered a contest. It invited all musicians in the community to write a song to celebrate the school's victory in the Class II basketball competition.

Sharon secluded herself for a week and composed a song. She recorded it and turned it in at the high school principal's office. We all expected her to do well, but she didn't even place.

The chairman of the judging committee announced the winner over the radio station. Everyone in the community knew that the judge and Sue were best friends. Sharon assumed that Sue had influenced her friend to reject Sharon's song.

The members within the church began to take sides in the issue. Some claimed that Sharon had just come in and taken over. Others spoke of Sue being jealous and thin-skinned. Sue began to take less and less interest in church. They both found their way to my study on different occasions to ask me to intervene and make the other person quit making trouble. I did not have any success in solving the predicament. The problem kept getting worse.

Sharon called for an appointment several weeks later. During the visit she kept fingering her purse and wouldn't look up.

"What's wrong?" I asked softly, recognizing that tears were close to the surface.

"My husband is being called back to the west coast. I, we, will be leaving in two weeks."

"Don't your folks live out there? You've told me that you miss them."

"Oh, yes, I'm not sorry to be moving." She waved a hand in the air. "It's just this thing with Sue. I can't leave without settling things."

THE BEAUTIFUL MUSIC

"Do you really think she had anything to do with your losing that contest?"

"No, it's just . . . things got out of hand. She said some things about me and I said some things about her, you know . . ."

"I see." We sat in silence for a moment. "Do you have any ideas about what you should do?"

"I'm going with my husband on a buying trip this week, and I thought I might get a gift for her. Do you think she would accept an apology?"

"Sue's a good person. If you are sincere, I'm sure she will listen." I prayed that she would be willing.

I suggested that Sharon visit one woman in the church who knew the other girl better than any of the others to get ideas for a peace offering. Two days later Sharon visited Sue. I do not know what they said to each other. Neither of them ever told.

When the church found out that Sharon and her husband were moving, they asked her to sing and play once more. She agreed to sing her last Sabbath with us.

Before her number, I announced to the congregation that it would be her last Sabbath with us. Then I publicly thanked her for all the contributions she and her husband had made during the short time they had fellowshipped with us. I nodded for her to go to the piano and sing once more for us. Instead she headed for the platform. Sue got up from her seat in the audience and walked to the piano.

We heard more than music that Sabbath. The congregation heard professionals and saw forgiveness in action. The church witnessed a family heal itself. The sad part is that the two women never made music together again. That was their last time to sing and play together. Maybe they will get to in heaven.

"Can God Still Love Me?"

I glanced at the clock before I answered the ringing telephone. It read 3:30. Sluggishly I tried to shake the sleep out of my voice before I picked up the receiver.

"Hello."

"Pastor, this is Jeanne. I, uh, we need you to come over right away." Tears filled her voice.

In that rural community most of the nurses at the hospital knew me from my visits there. Jeanne and her boyfriend, Tom, had visited in my home several times. She had been working the night shift now for several weeks.

"What's wrong, Jeanne?" I snapped awake.

"Tom's brother just died in an accident. Tom needs you. He's here now."

Hanging up the phone, I drove to the hospital. The night watchman quickly opened the door and pointed to the cafeteria where the couple were drinking coffee.

For the first time since meeting Tom, I watched him cry. However I could do nothing but cry with him. He came to my house to make the calls to his mother, who lived in another state, to tell her that his brother, her son, was dead.

Tom tried to soften the blow to his Adventist mother. I heard him explain that Jack had lost control of the Mustang and hit a tree. He grimaced when he told her, "Yes, Jack had been drinking." As I watched him cry again, I knew his mother must be weeping as well.

Jack and Tom Nelson had been raised as Seventh-day Adventists. During their academy years they had rebelled against the church and its rules. They had run away to the little logging community where I pastored, hoping to get rich. But they could not hide from their Adventist background, however, and let it slip to some mutual friends that they had once belonged to my denomination. Although I went after them, I couldn't get them to come back.

We were in the middle of a building program. Tom claimed that he was too busy to help out, but Jack had come on the site a few times. He did what we asked him to do and didn't say much. After he ate lunch he would go for a walk by himself. One of the young men of the church told me that Jack would smoke during that time. Another of the youths told me the smoke smelled like marijuana.

Figuring Jack had enough problems, I just tried to be his friend. I thought I had failed until late one evening he called and asked if he could come talk with me.

As he stood in my doorway, his messed up hair, wet from the rain, hung down over one eye. He brushed it back as he walked into the living room.

"What can I do for you, Jack?" He slumped down into the big chair like he had a heavy weight on his shoulders.

"I don't know, I just had to talk to someone." The words were slurred just a bit.

"Have you been drinking?"

"I had one drink. I had to. Otherwise I wouldn't have enough nerve to come here."

The young man looked at me with pleading eyes. I read a lot in those eyes. He waited to see if I would kick him out of my house. Jack wasn't drunk—just a frightened little boy of 24-short years.

"I'm glad you came. But why did you need to get your nerve up to see me?"

Life meant nothing to him anymore, he explained. He watched the other young people in the church and knew that he needed to change his life. But he had no hope!

"I've gone too far. I could never come back."

As I shared the gospel of Jesus Christ with Jack, he followed with his heart. I knew that something happened inside as we talked. Relaxing, he openly talked about his life and the things he had done wrong. My heart almost broke when he asked me a question about God.

"Can God still love me, even though I've done all these bad things?"

Once more his deep brown eyes searched my face for a trace of love and acceptance. "God," I silently prayed, "help me not to blow this. Help him to see You through me." The Lord gave me a confident smile.

"Jack, are you sorry for your past?"

"Yes."

"Do you want forgiveness?"

"Yes."

"Our Saviour has promised to forgive and help us to live clean new lives. Do you want help to do better?"

"Yes."

We knelt on the floor of my living room and Jack gave his heart to the Lord. Before he left he assured me that he would begin to change his life. He made no promises to be in church, only that as God helped him, he would follow. I really believe he meant what he promised God that night.

Two weeks later Jack was dead, without ever coming to church. I felt like I had failed. Jack, I believed, was lost forever.

At the airport I felt miserable as I watched Tom board his flight back home for the funeral. Such a waste. No hope! I drove home and closed myself away from everyone and prayed.

Then as God began to work on my heart I realized I was a sinner too. I had confessed my sins. Some days I had better control than other days. I did try to do better. More than once I had cried out to God as did Paul, "Oh wretched man that I am." I know that only by the grace of God did I continue and not give up. Every day I had to come to Him again for strength. I had not found perfection, yet I was willing to have God save me. What right did I have to expect perfection in others whom God wishes to save?

How did Jack live after he gave his heart to Jesus? I didn't know. But I did know that I had listened to the words that he had said that night, words that could mean the beginning of eternal life. Again, what right did I have to expect him to become a perfect Seventh-day Adventist before God would love and save him? Then I realized that I did not have that right! Jack would have needed to grow. It was God's part to determine how far that growth needed to be in two weeks, not mine.

What is righteousness by faith? I believe that Jesus' blood makes up for the sins I have confessed and am trying to let go of, sins that often take control of me, sins that will only be overcome through the power of God, sins that may take a lifetime to overcome. Jack's lifetime had been too short for God to have gained control of all those shortcomings.

Could it be that God really loved Jack, loved him enough to accept him in spite of the fact that not all his sins were under complete control? Could that faith that I hold for myself, hold for him?

That night I sat in my study all alone for a long time, these and other thoughts racing through my head. At last I found peace in trusting a merciful and just God. Maybe someone else needed that same peace. The telephone number of Jack's mother still lay where Tom had left it on my desk. I dialed the number.

"Mrs. Nelson," I began, "I had a visit two weeks ago with your son that I think you need to hear about . . ."

The Christmas Story

"Could you come by and see me?" Paul, the owner of a janitorial supply store, said on the other end of the phone.

"Sure, uh, is there anything wrong? The treasurer sent you the check for the supplies . . . ?"

"Oh," he answered, "it's nothing like that." He paused and then went on. "Let me ask you now, do you have anyone in your church who is not going to have a good holiday season this year?"

"Sure, doesn't every pastor? Usually we try to take care of them ourselves. What . . . uh, do you have in mind?" I tried not to appear too solicitous of some offer I thought he seemed ready to suggest.

"I know that your church helps people, I just want to help you help someone in a special way . . ."

"We have a program that we do every year," I began. "It's called Ingathering. Through it we collect money and then give out food baskets and things like that. These gifts also support the programs of the church all over the world. We can give you a tax receipt. Is this what you had in mind?"

"Not really. See, my family has been blessed this year and we want to help some other family have a good holiday."

"What kind of people are you looking for? I know lots of people who are hurting." I didn't like being on the spot like that.

"First of all, I want someone who is trying to do what's right. They can be working people who are without work. And they must have kids. Let's see," he continued, "they need to be short of funds and the kids are going to miss getting

THE CHRISTMAS STORY

many presents. Most people get the necessities. I want this to be the extras."

"Boy, Paul," I paused in mid-sentence, "that fits a lot of people around here. Let me get back to you in a day or so." I needed time to think.

"Sure, just stop in. Wait!" His voice shot out of the receiver. "Under no circumstances are they to know that this comes from me."

"Sure," I promised him. "I'll call you back tomorrow."

Quickly I got into the Christmas spirit. Still, how could I decide who needed a Christmas gift more than anyone else in the church? No one had ever given me free reign to supply gifts like that. My wife and I talked it over and could not come to a conclusion.

One of the church members worked for a city health organization. "Sally," I began, "I've got this special offer and I need advice to figure out how to handle it. Can you help me?"

"If I can." She had learned not to answer the pastor with a Yes until she knew what I wanted. "What do you need?"

The story poured out, with the exception of where the call originated. We discussed the people in the church and together we came up with a name. Now back to Paul.

I stood in his office and began to describe the person I had picked.

"She's a divorcée with two children. When her husband kept coming home 'stoned,' she had to kick him out. Within a short time a divorce followed and she got on welfare. One night, during prayer, she felt impressed to look for work. She took the children to her father. He's a struggling alcoholic, but promised to stay sober while she tried to find work. The only place hiring was the electric utility. 'Equal employment' meant that she would have to climb poles like the men. Well, she did, and has been working there ever since."

"Then how does she need help?" Paul interrupted. "They make good money!"

"Yeah, they do, but not enough to pay for the bills her husband and she had ran up while they were on drugs and things," I continued. "You know as well as I do that the apprentices don't make that much. Anyway, I heard that she is trying to pay off those bills. The only family she has is on welfare already, including her father. She can't leave the kids with him now, so she has to pay a baby sitter. Last week she told one of the members that the kids were not going to get much of a Christmas. The church will be seeing that they have something to eat, but we won't be able to help with the extras."

"That's exactly what I want." His smile almost broke his face. "I need to know what sizes the kids are and also what size she is. Get back to me as soon as you can."

My wife and another church member became the detectives and found out the information and delivered it to Paul the next day. During our conversation, I had promised to tell him how things went. He had interrupted me and told me his philosophy about that.

"Every year we help someone like this," he said. "My family is very well taken care of. During the holidays we like to think of assisting others. We like to think of people having real joy, and not knowing where it came from. I never want to know to whom, or to where these things go. Just knowing that someone is having fun is good enough for me and my family."

Nothing happened for a while. I feared that Paul was not serious about the whole thing. That thought left me depressed. Three days before Christmas he called again.

"Come on over, we have everything for you."

When I saw what he had done, I almost cried. Three garbage bags sat by the door of his office. The thin plastic was tearing in places, revealing brightly decorated packages.

THE CHRISTMAS STORY

Some long packages protruded out of the top of the bags. I must have looked stunned.

"You should have been with us," he brought me back to reality. "The whole family went wild. We tried to imagine what these kids would like. My boys have never bought presents for a little girl before, and they had fun pretending it was for a little sister. My wife picked out some things for the lady. Just in case they don't fit, we left the sales slips and the prices on the clothes so she can take them back and get some that do. Remember, she is not to know where these things came from."

I don't know what else he said that afternoon. All at once I had another problem. How could I get the things delivered without the woman knowing? Again I talked with my health organization member.

"Sally," I asked as I sat in her office the next morning, "do you know any policemen who would deliver these things for us without telling?"

"I sure do! This guy owes me some favors."

Within minutes she had an officer on her phone and the Santa Claus visit arranged for. The policemen would bring the gifts in uniform, so that she would know that it was not someone trying to put the make on her.

Two nights before Christmas a squad car with two off-duty policemen stopped on the cold street in front of her house. One of them went to the door and asked for Mrs. Candie Taylor.

"We have something for you," he said, motioning for the other officer who brought the first of the gifts to the door.

"What . . . who. . . you must have the wrong address! There's got to be some mistake . . ."

The officer handed her a note. It read, "These officers do not know where these gifts came from. The person responsible does not know who you are, either. People have been watching you and know that you are trying to do what is

MY FEET NEED WASHING, TOO

right. You will never be able to know where these things came from. Merry Christmas to you, Candie, and to Tammie, and to Jeff from people who care."

Candie never found out, though she tried. Taking the names and numbers of the officers, she called the precinct, but it knew nothing of the men delivering presents. She told the church members about the gifts, explaining that they could never have come from anyone in the church. "The toy guns for Jeff and the makeup kit for me. . . ." Her church family was as baffled as she.

Everyone who had a part in that Christmas story enjoyed it. Candie and the kids really had fun opening the gifts which seemed to come from nowhere; Sally, for helping me decide who to surprise; the officers who delivered the gifts, without knowing where they came from; Paul and his family for picking out the things and thinking of what that house must have looked like on Christmas morning.

But I had the most fun of all, because I knew everything and I couldn't tell until now. You see, Paul and his family are Jewish.

I Now Pronounce You Husband and Wife!

I knew that I had a problem as soon as I looked at the date on the marriage license. The couple could not legally get married for twenty-four hours. . . .

Have you ever noticed that those who are just married want to help others join them in the marital state? What you may not know is that those who have had marriage problems and get things fixed up also want to improve the marriages of their friends as well.

A young couple met me in my study and began to tell me of their problems. That one encounter turned into a series of visits. Members of the church would mention to me that the couple was hurting, and that I should try to help them get things together. Unfortunately I could never tell them that I was doing exactly that. Gradually the relationship between the two did improve and others noticed.

During one of our visits together, they asked me why the last pastor wouldn't marry them.

"What do you mean, he wouldn't marry you?"

"When we were married Jeff was not a member and the minister wouldn't marry us." Sue glanced down and away from both her husband and I. "I was a member and he wasn't."

I explained to them that all ministers have a responsibility to make sure that the relationship is one that God can bless. If there is a potential problem, the minister has an obligation to try to help the couple see how dangerous such a marriage can be. Should one be a member of one denomination and the prospective mate from another church, then the couple is setting themselves up for real problems.

Further, I told them that our church takes a stand that the minister should not perform such a ceremony. For me to marry a couple, they both should be members of the same denomination. If they are, then I can marry them, whether the denomination is mine or some other. "Does that make sense?"

She answered Yes though she didn't sound too convinced.

"The fact that the pastor couldn't marry you should not make you feel like a second rate person. It is only to help you know that you were taking a serious step. Won't you both agree that Jeff's not believing as you did in the beginning hurt your relationship?"

"Yes." This time it was Jeff who spoke. "I don't think that we understood all those things then. It's taken us a long time to get here. . . . I'm sure that we need God to be more involved in our relationship."

They needed more than just being members of the same church — they had to have God in their lives. With Him, things improved. Before long, church members began informing me how different Sue and Jeff were. I just smiled and said nothing.

After church one day, the couple asked me if they could talk to me alone for a few minutes. In my study Sue asked another question.

"Do you remember us talking about marrying people who are not members?"

"Sure, why?"

"Well," Jeff began, "we have these friends who want to get married, and they do not belong to any church. We told them how you have helped us and how they need to have God in their marriage. Would you talk to them and see if you can help them?"

"I'd love to. Have them give me a call."

A few days later two young people met me in my office. It

I NOW PRONOUNCE YOU HUSBAND AND WIFE!

was obvious that they had not talked to a minister very much. After a while they relaxed and we sorted out some of the facts. They answered every question I asked. Neither of them had any religious background. They considered themselves Protestants, but that was about all. However, both believed in God and explained that they had seen a difference in Jeff and Sue and wanted to have their relationship be the best that it could be.

I did not have an organized premarriage counseling series then, so I made one up as we went along. They seemed to be in a hurry, so we met more than once a week. I explained the laws of the state, how they needed to get a blood test first, and where to apply for the license.

Finally they set the date. It was to be a simple service at his mother's home for which they would invite twenty or so friends. The wedding would take place on Saturday evening with a small reception there in the house.

The Tuesday before the wedding I reminded them of the three-day waiting period before the license would be valid. "Be sure you get the license on time," I urged them strongly.

"Oh, we will." She smiled the innocent smile of a bride who looked almost overwhelmed.

Saturday evening my wife and I arrived at his mother's house. We got there early and became acquainted with her. They had some folding chairs set around with a couch in the middle. The bride was busy trying to make sure everything was in place.

I asked the groom for the license so that I could get most of it completed before the ceremony. The best man quickly handed it over to me. Taking it to the kitchen table, I began to fill in the blanks. The doorbell rang as guests began arriving.

As I finished all that I could, I looked at the date. Quickly I hunted for the groom.

"When did you pick up the license?"

MY FEET NEED WASHING, TOO

"Yesterday." He had a puzzled look on his face. "Why?"

"It's not valid till Monday! Look." I pointed to the paragraph which had Monday's date typed in as the earliest they could be married.

He didn't say anything for what seemed like hours. Then he called the bride over and we looked at it again. The date had not changed.

"We've got to go on with the wedding anyway," he spoke with authority.

She quickly agreed and then they both looked at me. Have you heard of your whole life passing before your eyes? My whole seminary experience flashed before mine. I remembered so clearly the words one professor used in warning us.

"Always make sure that you follow the laws of the state when you marry someone. If you make mistakes, you can be held criminally responsible, and how will that look on the official records the conference keeps?"

I could hear additional guests arriving. The couple was still staring at me. Swallowing, I batted my eyes, then looked at the license again. There was nothing I could do—or was there?

"Look, we can go through the ceremony . . ."

"Great," they interrupted me in unison, smiles once more on their faces.

"Wait." Their smiles vanished. "We have to make a deal here. Even though we go through the wedding tonight, it will not be legal. Therefore, tomorrow night at midnight we need to have the official wedding for the state. We can never tell anyone about this. Agreed?" I held my breath.

They glanced at each other and nodded. "Agreed."

"One more thing. I don't think I can pronounce you man and wife tonight. What I'll say is something like, 'I now introduce to you a couple who wish to be known from this night forward as Mr. and Mrs . . .'"

I NOW PRONOUNCE YOU HUSBAND AND WIFE!

"That's crazy," he said. "Who's going to know?"

"They will all know that something is fishy if you say that." She sounded angry.

"I'll do the best I can," I promised.

My wife knew something was wrong when I sat down by her on the couch. Jeff and Sue had joined her. One more time I looked at the license and prayed that the date would change, but it didn't. But then I noticed for the first time that both of them had given the same home address. It all became clear to me. Turning to Jeff and Sue, I asked, "How long have these guys been living together?"

Jeff counted on his fingers, turned to Sue and whispered for a bit, then answered, "Two and a half years."

I had never asked the couple that question. The bride and groom appeared at the door of the kitchen and the ceremony began. It was difficult to preach and think at the same time. In my understanding, they were already married in God's eyes. At the appropriate time I spoke the words they wanted me to say.

"I now pronounce you husband and wife."

The guests had no idea what the expressions on their faces reflected. But I did. It was a look of relief, joy, surprise, and love all mixed together.

Sunday night they arrived at my home at 11:30 p.m. We had crackers and cheese with 7-up to drink as a kind of mini reception. His mother had come along as they had told her about the problem. At exactly 12:01 a.m. we stood in front of the fireplace and I started the service with a prayer. Then turning to them I began, "Do you still take this woman to be your lawful wedded wife . . . ?"

"The Special Board Meeting Is Canceled"

During the announcement period at church one morning, I mentioned the need for a special church board meeting and urged every member of the board to come. In addition I stressed that the meeting was unavoidable. One hour later, after the closing hymn, before the benediction, I canceled that special board meeting. The board members shook their heads in disbelief.

Several weeks before I had preached a sermon calling for total commitment to the Lord. That there could be no halfway measure. I used an old illustration of an unhappy person, one who has just enough world in them that they can't enjoy the church, and just enough church in them so that they can't enjoy the world. I called on my congregation to make an unlimited commitment, to remove the world from their lives and be happy. Possibly in error, I suggested that if they didn't make this type of decision, they would never be happy in the church.

My Sabbath School superintendent called and talked to me about my sermon. Describing how it fit him, he went on to tell me how unhappy he found himself in the church.

"I have not always been a Seventh-day Adventist," he explained. "I grew up drinking beer. Ever so often I get the urge to sit back and relax with a drink. I know it's wrong, but I can't help myself."

"John," I asked, "do you think you will ever be happy in the world? You have enough church in you now that if you went back to that life, you will not find happiness."

"I know. That's where the problem is. I keep thinking I have to give up one side or the other. I have tried the church.

"THE SPECIAL BOARD MEETING IS CANCELED"

Now I think its time to try the world."

Silently I prayed for wisdom before continuing. How could I help him to see where what he contemplated would take him?

"Let's say you try to go that way, what would you do?"

"I have never really been a bad person. I don't think I would drink all that much. I didn't before. All I want to do is enjoy myself. I would like to go to shows, to dances, to do things that I know the church would not like for me to do."

"Doesn't the church offer the kind of things that replaced those interests you had before? I know that you enjoy the social activities this church has offered—at least those you attended."

"Yes," he said the word slowly, "but, it's just not the same. The excitement is not there. Things seem so dull in the church. It's just like you say, I have enough world in me that I can't enjoy anything the church has to offer. I'm not saying I wouldn't ever come back, or that I would stop coming. I just need some time to find out if being in the world would offer the happiness I want."

"John, what about your church office? You know that you can't possibly keep that office and do what you're talking about."

"I know, and that bothers me too. I guess I'll just have to make a complete break."

We talked for a while longer. Urging him to reconsider his position, I asked him to think about it for a while before he made a decision. His next Sabbath School was his best. I felt that maybe he was going to be all right. Then he telephoned me before the next week and announced his decision.

"Pastor, I just can't go on. I feel like a hypocrite. I want to resign from all offices starting right now. My assistant is scheduled to have Sabbath School this week. I should have done it before the last board meeting."

MY FEET NEED WASHING, TOO

"I'm sorry, John." I tried to think of something nice to say. "I will call for a special board meeting this next week. If you change your mind, let me know."

Feeling whipped, I went over what we had said again and again. Somehow I blamed myself for using that old illustration. What could I have said differently? What could I say now?

The next Sabbath I announced a special board meeting but did not tell the members why. John sat in the congregation with his wife and young son. "O, God," I prayed, "give me words today."

Preaching my heart out, I told of the love that God has for us, of His special gift of a Son to call us from a wicked world to be His children. I described the power available to us to change our lives. Then I closed with a silent prayer. "O, Lord, what more can I have said?"

During the closing song a deacon handed me a piece of paper. Opening it, I read: Cancel the board meeting. It was signed, John.

When I called off the board meeting, the members shook their heads in disbelief. I wish the story ended right there but it doesn't. It's not ended yet.

John stayed as Sabbath School superintendent for two more months and then resigned. Then he left the church and took his wife and son with him. Moving to a new district, I lost contact with him. A year ago a former pastor told me more of John's story. His son started drinking, too, but did not have the self-control that his father had. Prom night, the son with some others of his class had found John's beer. They got drunk. It led to a fight that resulted in the son's death.

John has now experienced both worlds. Which brought him the most happiness?

She Doesn't Tell Me Everything

Our son Tim attended a boarding academy. When the music weekend approached, my wife decided to go to the special programs. I could not leave until the afternoon and evening programs. Some members from our church gave her a ride to the academy that morning while I would come later.

Every congregation has a number of young people who do not go to a boarding academy for one reason or another and get their education at a public high school. I love those young people as much as I do those who have the opportunity to attend an academy.

Those who do go away to academy often remain good friends with those who remain home. Kathy, a young woman who went to public school, and Stan, one of those young men who attended the academy, had a thing going. At least that is what I thought. The couple always sat together when he returned home for the weekend. They were both well behaved and listened attentively to the sermon.

On the Sabbath morning of the music weekend, during Sabbath School, I noticed how lonesome Kathy looked with only a few of the youth her age attending church with her. The more I thought about it, the more convinced I became. Why not surprise her "boyfriend" by taking her with me that afternoon to the academy?

"Kathy," I asked her between Sabbath School and church, "I'm heading for the academy this afternoon, and coming back late tonight with my wife. Would you like to go along?"

MY FEET NEED WASHING, TOO

"Yes, I would. I'll ask Mom." She seemed happy for the chance.

After church we were on our way. I enjoyed visiting with her as we drove the three hours to the school and learned a lot about Kathy.

During the drive I kept thinking about how surprised Stan would be. I thought it would be nice for her to see the school as well.

As soon as we arrived on campus, we found my wife and Tim. They were surprised. Her reaction especially bothered me. Quickly I asked my son to show Kathy the school while I talked to my wife alone.

"Honey, is there something wrong? Do you think I shouldn't have brought her along?"

"No, there's nothing wrong with—me!" She said "me" kind of funny.

"What do you mean 'nothing wrong with me'?"

"I can't tell you now," she said with a slight smile.

While she would say little more, I found some comfort in the fact that she kept stressing that she had no problem.

Soon we caught up with Tim and Kathy and all walked together toward the boy's dorm to find Stan. The girl seemed to be enjoying the academy. Those students from our church who saw her there came running over to speak to her as we went across the campus. When we got to the dorm lobby, Tim excused himself and ran upstairs to get Stan.

A visibly surprised Stan came slowly down the stairs. The usual Sabbath afternoon group of young people were lounging around in the lobby. When they saw him approaching the very pretty Kathy, several of them began to call out their congratulations and other usual teenage comments. As the boy turned a deep red, I enjoyed myself. Stan would really owe me one, I thought.

A few minutes later several of the students started for the cafeteria for supper. Stan excused himself and took off. Now

SHE DOESN'T TELL ME EVERYTHING

I was surprised. *What gives here?* I thought to myself. Tim broke the silence.

"We might as well go and eat."

"Is Stan coming?" I asked.

"I-uh-think-he wants us to go on and eat," Tim replied slowly as if he were unsure how to say what he thought. We went to the cafeteria.

I kept waiting for Stan to come to supper and even suggested that we save him a place at our table. However he skipped the meal.

Once more I sent Tim to show Kathy the school. This time I demanded of my wife the truth.

"What is going on here?"

"OK, I guess there is no other way." She paused, took a deep breath, and went on. "Stan's Mom told me as one mother to another, and I was not supposed to tell anyone. She has thought of surprising Stan and bringing Kathy here, too. Stan told her not to."

"Why would any boy not want his girlfriend to visit him at school? That doesn't make sense?" The last was more of a question than a statement.

"OK, he has a girlfriend here too."

Now I knew why everyone was acting oddly. I guessed that Stan would not owe me one after all. Probably, I would owe him "one."

The boy had a lot of explaining to do that night to the two girls. I kept asking my wife why she hadn't mentioned it before.

"Stan's mom told me not to tell anyone. I think you are an 'anyone,' aren't you?"

"I guess so." At the time I still wished she had told me.

Things worked out between Stan and Kathy though it took a while. Within a few home leaves, they were once more sitting together in church when he came home. They even went places together though both have other friends as well.

MY FEET NEED WASHING, TOO

Neither one held anything against me either.

It was a simple thing, a conversation between two mothers about their sons. If my wife had mentioned it, I could have saved a lot of embarrassment for Kathy, Stan, and myself.

The boy's parents laughed with us when they found out. At the same time they learned what I already knew. You can trust this pastor's wife with any secret. She doesn't repeat them. There have been many times when I couldn't tell her everything either because of its confidential nature. Now, at least, I know how she felt.

"It's Too Bad He's Not Bringing Larry Home"

Sunday morning I drove up the winding drive to the Baker home. They had been taking Bible studies from me for several weeks. Mr. Baker's mother attended one of my churches and had asked me to study with her son. The couple were coming right along with the studies. As I drove up, I noticed several cars I didn't recognize in front of the house.

Mr. Baker walked out onto the front porch to greet me, even before I got out of the car.

"We've had some bad luck here. Come on in." Opening the door, he motioned with his hand.

Several people I didn't know sat in the living room looking at me. Mr. Baker introduced me to them.

"This is Mom's preacher. These are the parents of Jim, Larry's friend. Larry and Jim were arrested Friday night."

I nodded a greeting to the people sitting there and they returned it.

Larry, the Baker's oldest son, dressed like a hippie. At 17, he thought he knew everything. He hadn't been in trouble before, so I couldn't figure out why he would have been arrested.

"When we saw you coming up the drive I told everyone it was too bad you weren't bringing Larry home with you," Mrs. Baker joined in the conversation. "They have him in the county jail."

"What happened?" I asked. "What did he do?"

"He and Jim met a friend just back from basic training on his way to Vietnam," the father began to explain. "This army guy had the money, the boys had the car. They wanted something to drink, so they drove right up to the liquor store. The army friend ran in and bought a bottle. As soon as he came out and got in the car, the police drove up right behind and arrested them."

Explaining about the trial on Saturday afternoon, he told how the judge had released the soldier since he was going off to war. The two teens he sentenced to three days in jail for illegal possession of alcohol. The Friday night they had already spent there had not counted.

I did not know the judge personally, but I did know about him. He often would be caught walking the city streets drunk himself. The police covered for him, taking him home when they found him that way. The citizens of the city looked the other way, not wanting to get into more trouble if they were arrested for speeding or something. Needless to say, the Baker family thought it unfair to have their son jailed for being a minor in possession of alcohol.

We did not have a Bible study that morning. Quickly I drove back into town and went straight to the jail. The guard let me see the boys after he checked with the sheriff. Ministers have some privileges.

Larry and Jim both came to the door of the cell. Holding on to the black iron bars, they leaned as close to the openings as they could.

"How you guys doing?" I could tell they were miserable.

"Boy, it's good to see someone," Larry answered. "This is the worst thing that has ever happened to me."

Jim couldn't wait for the other boy to finish before he tried to talk to me.

"This is terrible. I don't think we deserve this. We didn't know it was illegal to have liquor in the car when we were in it." Somehow he didn't realize just how dumb that sounded.

"If we knew that it was wrong, we sure wouldn't have parked right in front of the liquor store," Larry added.

"You guys know that it is illegal for you to have liquor,

"IT'S TOO BAD HE'S NOT BRINGING LARRY HOME"

don't you?" They looked away before answering.

"Yea, I know," Larry said.

Later they admitted to me that they would have sent the army friend to get it in their car and would have drunk it somewhere else if they had realized they could go to jail. As we discussed their situation, they told how they wished they could break out. They explained that if the authorities would just unlock the door and leave it open, they would promise not to leave. The boys just couldn't stand having no choice in the whole matter.

I knew they needed to learn a lesson but thought there might be another way to teach them. Neither of the boys had a summer job. Maybe . . .

Back home I called my wife at her work and told her the story. She replied that sometimes she worked with the judge's wife at the hospital. He lived just around the corner from our house. After prayer I once more climbed into my car.

The house had tall white colonial pillars holding up the roof to the porch. The intricate front door reminded me of what I thought a fortress door would resemble. Very fitting for a judge, I thought. I pushed the doorbell button and heard chimes ring inside the house.

A moment later the door opened. A man stood there without a shirt. He didn't recognize me, either. As I was caught off guard by his dress, he quickly took charge.

"What do you want?" he demanded.

"I'm the pastor of the Seventh-day Adventist Church. My wife works with your wife. I live right around the corner. Yesterday you sentenced two boys to three days in jail. Could I talk to you about them?"

After studying me for a moment and determining that I was not a threat, he invited me in and we talked. I explained that my church had a building program going on. Currently we were digging the foundation and some of the work had to be done by hand. It was dirty and hard.

MY FEET NEED WASHING, TOO

"Sir, I think three days of hard labor digging a foundation would be a harsher punishment and one that I think the family and the boys could live with a lot better. Could you, would you consider releasing the boys to my custody and let me use them?"

Once more the judge looked me over. Did he think I was crazy? Was I insane to even suggest such a thing? Saying nothing more, I waited for his verdict.

"I don't think the sheriff will go for it." When he paused, I just waited. "Tell you what, you give me your telephone number. If the sheriff will agree, I'll give you a call."

I remember opening a can of tomato soup at home and trying to eat as I kept thinking of what might happen. The phone rang by the time I had half of the bowl of soup finished. The sheriff had agreed to my suggestion. The judge asked me to meet him at the sheriff's office in one hour. I never finished the soup.

An hour later a guard delivered the boys. Nobody had told them why they were being moved. When they reached the office, they were asked if they would work for me the three days instead of spending them in jail. Naturally they quickly agreed! The judge told me that I could take the boys home, that they didn't have to stay with me.

"I know where these boys live and if they don't perform, I'll get them later. Now get out of here!"

Once more that Sunday I drove up the drive of the Baker's home. This time I brought Larry home. The next three days found us digging and breaking rock for a church foundation.

"Where Did You Put Him, Heaven or Hell?"

The man on the other end of the telephone asked how much I would charge for his funeral. Assuming it was a crank call, I asked, "Are you thinking about dying?" Then I smiled to myself.

"You might say that," Mr. Thompson replied. "The doctors tell me I won't last six months."

Needless to say, I felt pretty bad about cracking a joke at a time like that. The next day I drove near the coast and visited the nursing home where Mr. Thompson resided. The red brick building seemed too quiet to please me.

The nurse showed me into his room. A night table beside his bed held a full complement of medicine bottles. Mr. Thompson lay on the white sheets with a tissue box by his head. He coughed and wiped his mouth before he could talk to me.

"My son is fixing up my will," he began. "I want a Seventh-day Adventist to have my funeral."

"I want you to know that there will be no cost for me to have your funeral. I get paid from the tithe and do not charge for these things."

"I'm glad you agreed to do it," he coughed and took a fresh tissue.

"I'm sorry that it will be necessary." I still had a hard time realizing that this man would talk so calmly about his impending death. "Are you a member of the Adventist Church, Mr. Thompson?"

"Not any more. I left the church several years ago."

The dying man paused and went back in time, taking me with him. Having been raised in a Seventh-day Adventist home, he eventually rebelled at all the rules and the requirements.

"When I married, I never told my wife anything about the Adventist church. She has been gone for a long time. My sons would never on their own call for a Seventh-day Adventist. That's why I want you to do things for me. I'm having it written in my will that you are to have the service."

We went over the things Mr. Thompson wanted said. He did not desire anything special, just a short service, no special music, the simple things an Adventist minister would say. I agreed to come back and visit him again.

He did not make the six months. Once more I drove down to the coast, this time to have the funeral. I believe that I was the only Adventist there. It went as well as one could expect.

On the way back I stopped off at the boat harbor where I often spent my days off. I had never been there in a suit before. A couple of crusty old fishermen friends saw me coming and invited me to join them on their fishing boat where they were working on an outboard motor.

"What are you doing here in a suit?" Joe asked.

"I just had a funeral and thought I would come by and check on the boats. What are you guys up to?" I leaned over and ran my finger along the rough edges of the aluminum propeller.

"Hey," George laughed out loud before Joe could answer my question, "I've always wanted to ask a Reverend this. Where did you put him, the guy you had the funeral for—heaven or hell?"

"I can tell you that," Joe replied before I could. "He put him in heaven, and I was not even there! You guys all do the same thing, don't you?" They looked at me, waiting to see how I would get out of that one.

"WHERE DID YOU PUT HIM, HEAVEN OR HELL?"

"No, I really didn't put him either place." They appeared surprised. "I put him in the ground."

That really brought out the questions. I explained that I did not have to make the decision concerning his eternal reward. Only God knew the ultimate destination of any man. I went back to the car and got my Bible. A few minutes later we continued our discussion.

Neither Joe nor George had much of a religious background though I knew that they both believed in God. You don't have some of the experiences they have had on the open seas and not know that some things can not be explained by just circumstance. Now I hoped that they believed in Scripture.

I showed them the simple truth of the Bible about the state of the dead. Joe shook his head with amazement.

"I've always wondered how these things fit together. This is the first time these texts made sense to me. I guess that's why I never went to church much. It seems so confusing."

"Joe," I said, "I believe that if religion doesn't work, it should be thrown overboard. I have studied this book. There are many things I don't understand yet, but I'm still trying." I prayed that they would not stumble over the idea of a minister not knowing everything.

We stopped our study with that. My friends never gave me another opportunity to discuss religion with them though I tried to continue to live a Christian witness in front of them. Maybe they will be ready to listen again sometime.

Many times I have thought about that afternoon. Close friends can strip away the facade and bring out the truth. I am happy that the Seventh-day Adventist message does have truth. Our faith makes sense. It will stand the test of investigation.

Furthermore, I am happy that Jesus has not asked me to

MY FEET NEED WASHING, TOO

decide who will be in heaven or hell. I am delighted that I can trust Him and wait for Him to deliver that verdict when He comes. Until then I am content to serve as His servant, a minister of the Seventh-day Adventist Church, because my faith makes sense!